TWO GIRLS CARRYING WATER IN A GOURD AND
AN EARTHENWARE POT

The woman behind carries a child on her back, one of whose little legs is
visible. The bracelets of the front girl are brass wire. This carrying habit
gives the women their graceful and dignified walk.

AFRICAN IDYLLS

PORTRAITS AND IMPRESSIONS OF LIFE
ON A CENTRAL AFRICAN
MISSION STATION

BY

DONALD FRASER, D. D.

AUTHOR OF "WINNING A PRIMITIVE PEOPLE"
"THE FUTURE OF AFRICA," ETC., ETC.

WITH INTRODUCTION BY

JEAN MACKENZIE

NEGRO UNIVERSITIES PRESS
NEW YORK

Originally published in 1923
by Fleming H. Revell Company, London

Reprinted 1969 by
Negro Universities Press
A DIVISION OF GREENWOOD PUBLISHING CORP.
NEW YORK

SBN 8371-2354-2

PRINTED IN UNITED STATES OF AMERICA

TO

MY WIFE

MY GAY COMPANION

THE FRIEND OF THE PEOPLE

INTRODUCTION

BY

JEAN MACKENZIE

HERE is a book by a man who was one of the founders of the Student Christian Movement in the British Isles, who has been since 1896 a missionary in Livingstonia, and who is, in 1923, Moderator of the United Free Church of Scotland. Of him it is agreed in Great Britain that he stands preeminent among missionary leaders.

Such a man—and indeed any devoted missionary—leads a double life. He is two men: he is of his own tribe, and he is of another tribe, dwelling in a stranger weather, speaking of less and greater things in another tongue, and knowing other fruits of the Tree of Life,—than his white brothers do. Standing before a white audience, the map that is hung behind him where he speaks can never mean to him the little it does to them,—for him it is a mountain and a river and a season; caravans make trails upon it and roofs are there with each a veil of smoke. When you hear a church bell he hears a drum; when you turn on an electric heater he remembers in his heart a friend of his, sitting on his heels above an ember that he blows to flame. Behind an audience of white faces he sees other faces—a sea of brown faces—it is the tide of the people of the Tribe of God that rises in Africa.

This extension of intimate human knowledge is the treasure of a missionary, and in the heart of an inarticulate man it is a hidden treasure. He just cannot tell you what he knows of primitive laughter, of the fears of primitive people and their sorrows, of their humble living and their arrogance, of their need of God and their appropriation of

INTRODUCTION.

His Word. Many an inarticulate missionary, reading this book, will envy Dr. Fraser his great gifts of expression— for here you may read what the wisest of them would be telling you. Here is the merchant who has travelled far, and he is displaying his pearl,—sit down with him by the fire of this little book, and he will take it out of his bosom. And then make search for his other books.

A Bulu once brought me a little song he had made in his own tongue; it is about the adventures of the Bulu who have gone among other Bantu tribes as missionaries.

And here it is:

> "If God finds a straight man
> And sends him to a far country
> He will return with a strange knowledge
> Of hills and rivers and forests and gardens!"

And for refrain there is this assurance:

> "Be at peace!
> You must stay with the work that you do!
> We see the work that you do!"
> Be at peace!

CONTENTS

LIST OF ILLUSTRATIONS

African Idylls

I

OUR AFRICAN HOME

THE station stands in a wide, open space surrounded on all sides by a broad belt of trees. The dense wood has been cut, and in its place a low, creeping dub grass has been planted, beloved of the herd of cattle that roams around in the months when the grass is green and succulent. Here and there are wide, spreading trees, and on both sides of the main roads avenues of oranges and mangoes, blue gums and cypresses, are gradually creeping up, promising to make a brave show in the future. Winds blow all day through the station during the dry season, bringing freshness and vigour that were strangers to the thick wood, and causing some irritation to the resident who loves a quiet peace, and not a little confusion to the modest native, whose dress is but a loose girdling of calico.

The houses are laid out in the pattern of a spade. At the cross on the top of the handle are the dwelling-houses. The handle itself is an avenue bordered with young orange trees, while round the blade of the spade stand the school, offices, hospital, and little circular brick houses for the boarders and others. In the centre a great cruciform church dominates the whole—a symbol of all that the station stands for. The main dwelling-house is imposing, indeed, for it is two storeys high, the only building so ambitious in all the tribe. Yet it is but a six-roomed house, with verandahs on two sides. Over the verandahs bright flowing " golden rain " has spread, until it covers the front with a screen of privacy.

A tennis court separates this house from the little cottage where the nurse lives with her flock of girl boarders. Behind her dwelling, in an enclosed compound, are one or two picturesque round houses for the accommodation of her girls, and all the courtyard is sprinkled with busy hens that lead about their broods of chickens, seeking invisible morsels, or running under the orange trees to shelter from a swooping hawk.

Our African Home

To enter the large dwelling-house you climb half a dozen steps, and stand on the lower verandah. The entire foreignness of the building slaps the African on the face. The raw stranger stands before these steps, and puzzles how he is to negotiate them. If he is an old person, caution conquers, and he climbs on his hands and feet like a monkey, for " he that is down need fear no fall."

Passing through the open door, you find yourself in a house with wooden floors. There are not many such in Nyasaland, for the white ant will soon discover them and reduce them to mud. But into this house our ubiquitous enemy cannot find his way, for thin sheets of lead are spread between the arches of the foundation, and these bar the progress of the exploring termite.

On the left is the dining-room, and before you opens the guest room, the best room in the house, seldom unoccupied, too. Scores of strangers have slept there, some of them coming unexpectedly out of the bush, strange in name and garments. They dash up on motor bicycles, or stride along bristling with sporting weapons, their great bare legs scantily covered with meagre shorts. All come sure of the hospitality that one white man shows another in this kindly land. Here, too, have dwelt friends who came accompanied by an army of carriers, with boxes battered by many a mile of rough travel, and packed with food and cooking utensils for the long road, and with the garments of civilization.

One day there was borne in a poor traveller, sick unto death. He and his mate were on a long trek that was to lead them all through Africa, right up to the Nile, looking for gold and precious stones. But miners' phthisis, the price of Johannesburg gold, had gripped him on his way, and in utter pain and weariness he had been carried here.

From the day he found himself lying between clean sheets, washed, fed, nursed, his soul flowered with gratitude and love. As the weeks passed, hope alternating with dark forebodings, while watchers sat by him through the long days and nights, he wound himself round the hearts of everyone. He called the missionary " Daddy," and the doctor and nurse " Little Mother." Every small service was a radiant gift, calling for the most winning smile of thanks. And so he passed, after a life full of excitements and rough tumbles, into the calm of God's Presence.

From the lobby a stairway leads to the upper

Our African Home

floor, with its bedroom, sitting-room, and little study. What an adventure it is to climb into these heights! A Headman comes with his inevitable followers, and asks to see the house. He stamps up the stairs, thumping and slithering from step to step, with a shy, half-frightened smile, and is led out to the verandah. At first he hangs back, fearing that the planks will not bear him, and when at last he ventures out, and sees below him his humble followers, with simple delight and wonder he calls on them to look at his great adventure. They answer with shouts of awe, especially when he tells them the names of the hills and country that lie before him, quite visible though these are to those squatting on the ground. As he passes through the study, and sees the shelves filled with books, he is silent, as in the presence of potential magic.

But what attracts me to this house? It is not yet twenty years old, but it is haunted by ghosts. I have only to close my eyes, and I see them in every room. Jolly sociable ghosts, sitting out on the verandah, smoking innumerable pipes, and telling yarns. Rowdy little ghosts, whose feet run from room to room, and whose calls and shouts allow no peace. Sad, anxious ghosts of mothers, watching through sleepless nights lest little sunbeams slip away, and leave the world so cold and dark. And the house is dearer to one because of the pain that has mingled with its joy. For in Africa the days and nights when battles are fought with death seem to be more frequent and more sudden than in Britain. Homes here are shrines, and sacred for the memory of these fierce struggles. You feel the mingling of light and shade as soon as you enter this land of sunshine and tragedy. Steaming up the waters of the Zambezi, the first place you look for is Shupanga, and the red-tiled house where Livingstone watched by the side of his wife, and saw her life ebb away; and next that baobab tree under which he laid her to rest, thus setting up another African milestone, before passing on to his long and patient travel. If you have had some such experience, the rooms of your house will be for ever sacred to you. The appeal of this house to me is that every room has been full of the shouts of happy children, has had the light and love and society of friends, and has some association, too, with days and nights of terrible dread.

How the children danced and yelled that Christmas Day when Santa Claus descended so successfully from a man-hole in the ceiling! For a long time they passed with awe below the little square trap-door, never doubting that his white beard might again peer through the opening. Until that other Christmas when he appeared, hobbling across the golf course, clothed in scarlet dressing-gown, and wearing his snow-white locks. The children watched his coming from the verandah with growing excitement, and saw him pass benevolently through the herd of cattle browsing there, until he suddenly became aware that the bull of the herd was attracted by his brilliant gown. Then age and all the dramatic proprieties were forgotten, as he fled, with unexpected agility, gown streaming in the air, locks and beard scattered to the wind, an excited bull drawing nearer and nearer to his flying heels.

In the warmer lands in Africa the verandah is the most frequented part of the house. It serves as sitting-room, dining-room, and sleeping-room. But in this high plateau it is not so completely the centre of life. For, from May to July the cold is pretty severe, and we are glad to sit over fires within the house in the evenings. But when the days grow hot again we breakfast outside behind the screen of creepers, and all the year long we sleep on the upper verandah with stars watching, until the dawn and all the sounds of wakened life stir us again.

It is on the verandah we sit with our guests in the cool nights when dinner is over, and all work laid aside. The stars are bright, and a clear moon shining. The woods, billowing for miles away in gentle hollows and rises, lie in a soft grey light. Twenty miles away the hills are dimly seen in most delicate haze. From the trees around us there is a constant croaking of frogs, and the delicious love gurglings of the doves and pigeons, and occasionally the long, drowsy call of the eagle owl. Out from the depths of the wood there may come the melancholy howl of the hyena, or the strident bark of a fox. The wind that blew all day has fallen asleep, and the wood is awake with voices of the night.

In such a delicious setting, the yarns sometimes tumble out in full stream. Night after night a prospector has been telling great stories of the days when he was a scout with the Boers, and followed De Wet in his long rides, stories of Colenso, and Magersfontein, and Mafeking, all from the Boer point of view. Crisp, exciting yarns with no wasted word, of furious rides, sharp skirmishes, and wild

The Loudon House

Roofed with buff-coloured tiles, raised on arches isolated with lead to
protect it from white ants.

The Loudon Church

A lad may be seen on the shingled roof. The Church holds about 2500 people
who are seated on mats.

orgies, too. Then stories of Tierra del Fuego, and ranching, and sharp work with six-shooters.

Again, a Government official who has served in Palestine and the Sudan has held us with growing interest, as he described, with unusual powers of vivid picturing, life in the Holy Land and scenes in the Sudan, the slimness of the Egyptian officials and the plans for making a great rich possession of that once so harassed land.

From distant Bihé an American Missionary and his wife have dropped in, and have stories to tell of the lands they have passed through in their months of travel, and their experiences of the incredible blocking power of the Portuguese who so effectively arrest all progress in Africa. Another has come from Mashonaland in the south, arriving with his wife one night on donkeys after we were all asleep. They had jogged on hour after hour, always expecting to arrive suddenly among us, and hoping that in the dark they might not miss the path that leads here. And yet another riding on the carrier of a motor bicycle, who has passed across Africa three times, and has gathered much knowledge. We pump all our guests hard, and rivers of new things flow to our delight and refreshment.

Our African Home

Government officials, planters, soldiers, traders, Catholic fathers, apostles of some wondrous new American religion bent on a poaching expedition, D.B.S.'s—i.e., "distressed British subjects—lady travellers; Greeks, Poles, Israelites, Italians, English, Irish, Scots—all pass this way, and find some shelter, and have some rich gift of experience, or character, or story that makes their visit memorable.

All evening a senior missionary has been sitting very quiet, but with that sympathetic silence that is perfect company. A short laugh, or a fixed sober look has revealed plainly enough that he is a thoroughly interested member of the group. At last he is asked to tell about his late curious experience with lions, and he tells this story, looking over his spectacles with humorous eyes, laughing now and then at the absurdity of the situation. His hands touch one another at the finger tips, and quietly tap each other by way of emphasis.

One day there came news to his lonely station in North Rhodesia that an old hunter had been crushed to death by a wounded elephant. Before he had died he had scribbled a note to the nearest magistrate: "Caught at last. Going home," and now

Our African Home

our friend was going off in the early morning to bury his mangled remains. He had a walk of three or four miles before him, and two native lads accompanied him. They carried no weapons, only their long walking-sticks. The road was a broad, hoed one, flanked on both sides by high grass. Silently, without a word of conversation, they pursued their journey, our friend's eyes studying the ground. We all credit him with hunting for language roots, but possibly his mind was occupied with no deeper thoughts than of the breakfast he had just eaten. At any rate, he and the two natives suddenly became aware that two lions were sitting on the road before them, their heads looking at the travellers, their tails swishing back and forward. The boys followed, breathing hard, but not a word passed. Nearer and nearer they came to the beasts, yet there was no slackening in our friend's meditative stride. The curious indifference of the travellers was more than the monarchs of the forest could understand, and they got up, turned tail, and bounded out of sight round the next turning. Our friend continued his regulation stride without a break, the natives padding softly after the metallic clatter of the European boots. No word was spoken, not even an exclamation uttered, and the missionary continued his patient hunt for that elusive language root.

So they swung round the next bend of the road, and there were the lions again guarding and closing the road, watching the travellers, and swishing their tails in angry bewilderment. But the march went on, not a moment of hesitation, not a slackening of the steady tramp, and not a word spoken. It was all so strange to the lions. Had these men never heard of their reputation, or trembled at their earth-shaking roar? Apparently not, for the grey-bearded man was only looking over his spectacles, and steadily tramping on.

It was altogether overwhelming. So up jumped the beasts again, and bounded on in front, and a third time sat down to wait for the terror and flight that ought to follow. But the missionary tramped on, followed by his quaking companions. Nearer and nearer they drew to the two lions. At last the strain proved too great for the unexpected terrors of the road, and with an angry growl they rose and bounded away into the grass, never to return to that road. As the sound of their bounding flight in the crackling grass died away in the distance, the two natives drew a long breath, and said : " The Word of the Lord ! "

That was the only sound of human speech that passed between these travellers in those strange, intense moments. Nor through the rest of the journey was any comment made on the incident.

I felt that one word only needed to be spoken by our silent Scottish friend. He should have looked over his specs, and said in good vernacular to each of his native companions, " Chatterbox ! "

II

A SCHOOL IN CENTRAL AFRICA

A FEW yards outside the untidy village, if you follow a roughly hoed road, you will come to a large rectangular house of poles and mud, roofed with grass. This is the village school. It is a fairly new building, much superior to any other in the neighbouring villages, where there are few more ambitious than the ordinary African round hut. For this one is not African at all in appearance. There is nothing round in its construction. It is built with straight lines and right angles, two geometric symbols that are utterly foreign to anything African, or indeed natural. For circles and curves are more like the flowing moods of Africa. She thinks and acts without sharp and sudden angles. She rounds her corners, for space is unlimited ; she never leaps her obstacles on the path, but turns aside and encircles them, for time seldom presses.

The house is perhaps sixty feet long, and sixteen

wide. The heavy roof is thatched with grass, and there are little openings along one side of the building which serve as windows. The opposite side is closed against the prevailing wind, which numbs the naked pupils in the cold season, and plays tricks with dust and loose papers all through the hot. An open doorway at one end, without frame or door, provides an entrance. Step inside, and you will find a long room with a solid line of large trees set deep into the ground, and serving as pillars to support the roof. There is no nail in the structure, and no material which cannot be found in the neighbouring bush. The rafters and the thatching are tied with bark rope. The walls are roughly plastered with mud, and decorated with bright-coloured clays. The floor is beaten and rolled earth. One or two logs raised on forked sticks serve as seats for the select of the congregation or school, and, at the far and rather dark end of the house, there is a raised platform of beaten mud with a little table made of four forked sticks which support a tray of reeds bound by bark. On the table lie a Zulu Bible, a school roll book, and a few other papers and some slates.

The wall behind the platform is ornamented with

A School in Central Africa

papers containing programmes of work, a syllabus of Bible lessons, and a small blackboard.

There you have the educational establishment in which the dim and flickering flame of learning is kindled and maintained by weak and poorly directed effort, and in which the Christian religion is daily taught.

There is not much there to impress the European, except the crudeness and simplicity of the outward symbols of education. Yet such a school-house is as impressive to the village as the best County Council school is to the Londoner, and as far above his ordinary dwelling-house. What is better, he has a personal pride in it that the Londoner may never have in his stone palace. For with their own hands, and by their own skill and industry, the villagers have built this house. They have used but two instruments—the native made hoe, and axe. On their bare shoulders they have carried from the wood every pole for the walls and roofing, and with their own hands as trowels they have plastered the walls within and without, and with round stones from the brook they have rolled the hard floor. The final decoration of the walls has been the pride of the pupils, and the crude representation of antelopes, and leopards, and fashionable European ladies which brighten the walls, are the highest expression of pictorial art their tribe has yet attained to.

What men have fashioned for themselves, and built at cost of sweat, and thought and talk, is far more precious than the costliest result of money purchase.

But unfortunately there is no guarantee of long enjoyment of all this labour. In five or six years the villages will change their site, and the school will be left stranded in a wilderness of thick growth, the fruit of a soil which the villagers have fertilized for years, and have abandoned, while the rain and sun have diligently woven the thick entanglement. Now it has become inconveniently far for the undisciplined little children, so much the masters of their own life, to come to morning school, and if the attendance is not to go hopelessly down, or be maintained only by a vigorous system of whipping up every morning, the building must be removed to a more convenient site.

So, after half a dozen years of pride, it begins to fall to pieces by the action of white ants and rain, and is not renewed, for already the poles of a new

A School in Central Africa

academy are being stuck into the ground near the new village sites.

Sometimes we have encouraged the people to erect a brick building. These require much stimulus, many visits, constant superintendence during their erection. But not long after all the labour has been rewarded by a magnificent structure in bricks and clay, the villagers have followed their ancient practice, and shifted their huts to a new site, and lo ! the palace of bricks stands alone in the bush with no people to warm it, and no congregation to give it life. Then the European says that never again will he spend so much useless energy in works for so temporary a purpose.

But as time and labour abound in Africa the demands that the erection of a new pole and mud school-house make on the villagers are not so great as to be grudged.

On such a school as I have described the dawn has broken, and the cocks in the villages are stridently awake, when Daudi tumbles out of his little hut in which he has slept lying on a reed mat spread on the hard floor. A broad piece of calico has been his only blanket, but it was drawn so tightly over his head that the wonder is how he found air to breathe. His feet were stretched out to the open wood fire that smouldered and flickered through the night.

Now habit and the chill of the morning have wakened him, and he has crept out by the low door into the open air, carrying with him an ember from the fire. Gathering a few small dry sticks together, he vigorously blows the ember into flame, and having started the little fire he sits down on his haunches, hands spread out over the little flame, and sleepily blinks in the sun. Two or three other lads join him from neighbouring huts, and, with backs bared to the rays of the rising sun, they sit quietly thawing.

A small boy is summoned, and told to blow the call for prayers. He takes down from the thatch a large twisting kudu horn, and pours a little water into it. Then, mounting a neighbouring ant-hill, he blows long piercing blasts from his horn.

Meanwhile Daudi has fetched a little gourd filled with water, and is busy with his morning ablutions. He pours a little water into the hollow of his left hand, skilfully saving every drop, and then, laying down his gourd, washes both hands. Next he pours

A School in Central Africa

a little into his right hand once or twice, and manages to get the whole splashed over his face and into his mouth, which he carefully rinses. Then he sits down to dry, the fresh air acting as towel. His toilet is complete.

There is not much in all this to distinguish him from the ordinary villagers. Yet Daudi is the head teacher of the school. But there is this great mark. He is cleaner, and before he left his hut he prayed.

For indeed Daudi is the interpreter of God to the village, and although he has not yet learned deeply himself he has in his house the key to all mystery, a Bible, which is a speaking book to him; and his daily conduct, led and moulded by higher thoughts than are known to any in his village, is a guide for others towards the new life that Christianity creates.

A few men and women are straggling out of the village, and are making their way to the village school. It is now a church, and morning worship is to be held therein. Daudi had taken his seat along with the other people, and when all seem to have assembled he gives out a hymn, which is vigorously sung. Its music is unfamiliar to

A School in Central Africa

European ears, but it is characteristically African. Probably it is an old song tune rescued from oblivion, and made to live again as music for God's praise. The people sing in harmony, and without books, for the words are almost as familiar as the tune.

Then a portion of scripture is read, and, if Daudi is in voluble mood, it is expounded shortly. He leads in prayer, and closes with the Lord's Prayer. After a few moments' silence the congregation disperses, the women making off rapidly to resume their endless household duties, and the men stand about having a lazy gossip before they go back to the village.

Now the day has fairly opened, though it is only a little after six o'clock. All nature is in full morning song, and village life is in vigorous volume. Nothing is done in a hurry in this land, yet for an intelligent man like Daudi there is enough to occupy a fairly full day.

Before half an hour of leisurely preparation has passed the twisted horn is sending its long, insistent blasts through the wood, and in three or four villages the children are being rounded up by their seniors. Little Vukeya and the other girls of her age, who have been idling under the eaves of their mothers' huts, are now shouting to one another to come to school. The parents order them sharply to be off, but have little expectation of being obeyed. The children will go only if they are disposed to go, or are chased by a senior lad, or a school monitor.

As for the boys, Zondwayo, and Isaiah, and Joshua, and Noah, and all the patriarchs, they have already been busy in the cattle kraal milking the cows into unwashed wooden vessels, and must now have at least a cat's lick at their faces. Half a dozen of them are really keen to learn, the others have tired of a listless attendance at school which has never lifted them out of the syllable class. But the Old Testament patriarchs are determined to take the others with them, so with much shouting, and rushing here and there, the zealots pursuing, the slackers dodging, most of the youngsters are finally swept into the stream that flows its winding course towards the school, chattering as it goes.

Daudi and his monitor are waiting for them, and draw them up in two long, descending lines, according to their stature, to give them a few minutes of

A School in Central Africa

" dirrill." I fear the efforts, energetic though they are, may seem a caricature of military or Swedish drill, but they serve to put some physical energy and order into the mass. And here you may observe a curious thing—that while most of the common English words which the teachers use are spoken with a distinct Scottish accent, and a rolling emphasis on the " r," the military commands have an English twang, for have they not come by way of the " Askari," who have been exercised by English officers ? In the school you will hear the teachers call for the " Thirrrd Rreaderr." But on the playground he will shout " Left Tu'n," if indeed he succeeds in avoiding the *l* and *r* pitfalls, and does not call " Reft Tu'n." But when the drill is over, and the march in single file into the school begins, I'll guarantee that he calls " Reft, Light, Reft, Light," to keep his pupils in step.

You won't be long in school, if there is an English class there, until you find that here is the greatest difficulty in our absurd language. For the African can hardly distinguish between the *l* and *r* sounds. And he will see no humour when you assure him that you do not buy lice,

A School in Central Africa

but rice, and the cow does not eat glass, but grass.

But I am anticipating, and have only succeeded in getting the pupils marched into the school. There they stand in line facing the far end, still marking time, patiently waiting until my explanation is over, and until with a stentorian voice Daudi shouts: "Front tu'n! Sit down," and they all squat.

A hymn is sung. The volume of sound is immense, if it is a popular hymn. The tune is "Glasgow," an old wailing Scottish tune, and the trills are given with emphasis. The patriarchs are in full cry. Their mouths are yawning gulfs, edged by rows of shining teeth. Their eyes glisten with the verve of joyful sound, and their bodies sway to the cadences of the music. You glance at the words to see what has put such soul into the singing, and find they are singing a translation of the Forty-Second Psalm:

> "My tears have unto me been meat
> Both in the night and day."

But no sense of incongruity disturbs Daudi's solemn precenting.

THE AUTHOR IN HIS OFFICE IN LOUDON

BREAKFAST ON THE VERANDAH

Mr. W. P. Livingstone sits on the left with the author's family.

A School in Central Africa

When the song is over, Daudi leads in prayer, and then comes the Bible lesson. It is fully expounded, with many questions framed to elicit the least possible thought, and to suggest the answers unmistakably. For the teacher speaks thus : " Who was the Mother of Jesus ? Ma——" And the pupils answer, " Mary." Where was He born ? In Bethle——" And the pupils answer, " Bethlehem." The learned European pedagogue tears his hair in despair, and suggests that questions should be given to call out the thinking powers of the pupils ; but Daudi feels that his are framed to show their great intelligence.

The classes are now divided up, and soon the school has the sound of intense activity. In the first class the whole bunch of naked urchins are soon shouting their syllables in unison. There are some who can repeat the great wall sheet from end to end without a mistake, in a pleasant chant, but cannot distinguish a single syllable standing in unsupported isolation. But there are a few who have found out that this sheet is not a song, but a chart of sounds each separate and distinct. This is the insidious evil of the whole school, this parrot memorizing, and all your years of wise and penetrating inspection and instruction have not rooted it out. In the first reader there is a blind boy at the head of the class. Daudi points out his great genius and skill. He stands with a book which he cannot see in his hand. He has learned every word by heart, and can read fluently when his turn comes, and correct any slip another makes, and spell without a mistake. For he, like many another, believes that memory is the key to learning

You stand and wonder how progress is possible. How can any find the way to real learning by such a hapless system? Yet year by year the school is producing its readers, and lads and girls are entering into the wonderful land where pure laws and more orderly lives are formed, and where God walks. For though many a pupil has wandered into blind alleys, Daudi himself has found the straight avenue and is leading onwards, whether they follow or no.

Two or three hours complete the lessons for this junior school, and then, with a repetition of the Lord's Prayer, the pupils noisily disperse to their occupations, the girls to help their mothers with pounding, and drawing of water, the boys to spend the day out in the wide green valleys, herding the cattle and goats till the sun grows red in the western horizon.

But in the afternoon a very serious school of senior lads and girls gathers. They are the advanced pupils, some of whom are now stumbling through the English Readers, taking enormous mouthfuls of the foreign words which seem to have so little relation between their sound and their appearance in print. Huge sums of money are subtracted and multiplied, with a terrible earnestness, every pupil feeling that he is a potential storekeeper or teacher with fabulous wages in front of him, if only he masters the intricacies of arithmetic. Most of these senior pupils have now reached some stage of Church standing. For one of the glories of living religion is that it seems to awaken the mind as well as the soul. And one of the first fruits we find in Christian folk is an eager desire to learn more fully the arts which are taught in school.

At last the evening sets in, and Daudi has leisure to sit with other men at the kraal gate and talk of all the stirring events of the quiet villages round him. But before the village retires to sleep he gathers them again in a clear space within the village, and worships God. And thus having begun, continued, and ended his day in most holy service, he lies down to sleep, the cloth drawn tightly over his face, and his feet warmed by the glow of the undying fire.

III

AN AFRICAN BEADLE

BEADLES are a peculiar race both in Britain and in Africa. Their office seems to create forms and growth that can only be produced in this soil. No beadle is complete until he has developed his own peculiar type, which must differ from that of all others. Perhaps there is something in Presbyterianism which tends to this curious growth, for no sooner has a staid and serious beadle been planted than strange branches begin to sprout from him.

We have a delightful beadle in Africa, whose name is Their Master. He is growing old now, though he has only held his office twenty years, and his grandchildren are multiplying about him. Often, when he is unable for his work on Sundays, one of his numerous sons appears to take his place. The first time I took notice of him was when we were building a large brick church at Hora entirely by free labour. On the ant-hill from which we were hewing clay for brick-making, a little hairy man, clad in nothing but a scrap of loin-cloth, was wielding his hoe with great deligence. Now and then he stopped to take a big pinch of snuff, or to ask for one. Then he would sit down on his haunches, and make jocular remarks to the crowd of workers who swarmed on the monster ant-hill.

On the Sunday following he was at church, with a great Zulu Bible and hymnbook in his lap. As I was going to some distant villages, I said to him that I would not be able to preach in the afternoon and he must learn to do more than to break ant-hills, so that he might help me.

" What sort of work should I do ? " he asked.

" Why not take the afternoon service ? " I said, not thinking it likely that he, a mere labourer, would even think of it, when there were teachers there who often preached. But he was more willing than I thought, and at once agreed to take my place. Public speaking has few terrors for the African, for he is accustomed to it from his youth up. The public hearing of court cases, when the witnesses and principals have unfettered opportunity for testifying, are the great and constant entertainment of the people.

An African Beadle

When I returned in the evening my wife told me that Their Master had spoken well, though with more nervousness than is usual in the African. From that day he became one of our regular village preachers, going forth on Sunday afternoons to one of the surrounding villages. Soon after I learned that he was the recognized religious leader of his own village, and that his sterling character had made him a kind of village priest.

One day he came to me to tell me how his village headman, who was a catechumen, had grown indifferent to his wife, and at last had neglected her altogether. This hurt Their Master's sense of Christian duty. So he had inveigled the headman into his wife's hut and induced him to sit down and talk to her. Then he had slipped out and barred the door, and left the couple all day within to make one another's acquaintance and find out the excellences of one another's characters. Strange to say, husband and wife did not resent this heroic measure, and from that day they lived happily together until death parted them.

As soon as the great church at Loudon was completed we found it necessary to appoint a beadle to care for the building, and Their Master was chosen.

47

An African Beadle

His duties were light enough, but he soon learned the art of spreading them over the entire day. When I suggested at any time some extra work, he was always able to point out that he had no unoccupied hours. He swept the building, and, seeing the floor was made of polished mud and there were services every day, and considerable congregations on the Sunday, the sweeping and dusting did give some work. Then he was expected to keep the windows clean, but in a smokeless land that was no great task. When the time for recolouring the walls with clay-wash came each year at the close of the rains, you could find him all day long perched on a little ladder, with a tiny bit of rag, rubbing and polishing gently, as if he feared his hand would go through the glass. Then his window-cleaning would be extended for weeks.

To see him sweeping the paths surrounding the church was a lesson in the art of prolonging a task. He squatted down, and swept diligently, but leisurely, against the wind. A strong puff would send some leaves back over the place he had already swept. With a grieved look of remonstrance against the freaks of an unfriendly wind, he would watch the leaves until they settled, and then, following them slowly, he would gather them up and replace them whence they had come. Squatting down, he resumed the interrupted work. All day this steady pursuit of frolicking leaves would be continued after every strong blow, and the labour of sweeping was converted into a Herculean task.

As the years have grown upon him he has not acquired the art of speedily finishing his jobs, but has rather increased the necessary time. You come into the church some day and see, by the presence of his best cloth and snuff-box on a pew, that he is somewhere in the building, yet as perfect silence reigns you are at a loss to discover where he is. By and by the old man comes along, and sits down beside you. After he has taken a snuff he slowly remarks that the church is breaking to pieces. If you have not yet learned his ways, you start up, alarmed, and ask where the ruin has begun.

" Over there in the transept the wall has broken down," he deliberately remarks. You pull him to his feet and with some concern hurry him along to show you where the trouble is. But he moves undisturbed and silent, until he brings you to the place, and then he points out that a little piece of the mud plaster has fallen off.

An African Beadle

" Is that all? " you ask, with a feeling of relief.

" Yes. Didn't I say that the wall was breaking down? " he answers, mildly indignant that you did not grasp the nature of the damage from his plain statement. And then he eyes it with his head to one side, and opens what he hopes will be a quiet, prolonged discussion about the method of replacing that piece of mud plaster, and when it will be done, and who will do it. There is subject enough for a pleasant half-hour's business conversation here. And when you leave him, after saying all you have to say in half a minute in your silly European haste, your last sight of him is standing with his head cocked to the side, eyeing the broken plaster, while a pinch of snuff slowly travels up to his nose to aid his reflections.

Now, Their Master is a good man, and in that lies his priceless value. To have him caring for and loving the church, and pervading it with the atmosphere of goodness that surrounds him, is a great asset. In the early Sabbath morning you may walk into the church and see him laying down the long mats on which the people are to sit, and rejoicing if that day is to see a great congregation because of some special event, though he knows that the crowds who may come will immensely increase his own work. He is jealous for the honour of God, and the more his church is frequented the more he sees God glorified. But the work began this morning before the mats were laid, for he has been warming and airing the church by his prayers. The preacher who comes may know that the old man has been praying here in the early hours that God will give a message to his minister and find a way into the heart of all the worshippers.

When the preacher waits in the vestry before the service begins, the beadle joins him after he has finished ringing the bell, a quiet, unobtrusive figure clothed in white, amid the crowd of little boarders who form the choir. Before they sing " The Lord bless thee, and keep thee," the beadle leads in prayer. There is always a pleasant surprise of metaphor in his prayers, though sometimes he is apt to disregard the waiting congregation and continue in prolonged prayer, to the confusion of all exact time-keepers.

Sometimes his whole prayer is a string of pictures, a little shocking at times to the refined sense of the European, yet not more so than many of Samuel Rutherford's luscious images of the love of Christ.

An African Beadle

To-day the picture is of a garden, and the hoe is uppermost. He describes the soil of the congregation, the weeds and neglect that have spoiled the garden. Then he speaks of the Spirit of God, Who has been carving out for Himself a long hoe handle and fixing the iron into the shaft, and prays that the Spirit may take the preacher into His hands, as a well-made hoe, and turn the soil, and destroy the weeds, and prepare a rich, fruitful garden.

Another day he thinks of himself and the people as helpless little children. God is a mother who takes the children to her breast, and gives the milk of life and refreshment. Again, God has gone forth as a hunter, and the people are the wild beasts of the forest, and He has His quiver full of arrows. So he prays that God may take the preacher as a bow into His hands, and stretch the string, and shoot the arrows till the wounded and slain are lying here and there. And then the Hunter must come as the Healer and life-giver, applying His medicine, until the wounded rise healed and tamed. Or again he drifts away into Scripture story, praying its detailed application to our present needs.

From such an atmosphere of praise and prayer

An African Beadle

we pass into the church prepared for worship, and with some sense of God over all.

Sabbath is the beadle's great day. He knows the honour of being a doorkeeper in God's house. In the morning you will find him in the class of Sunday School teachers, sitting with the others, going over the lesson which is to be taught afterwards to the children, for he is a Sunday School teacher. In the afternoon he is always among the village preachers who go out to the neighbouring villages to hold open-air services, for he is a preacher, too. Between services you may find him sitting in a quiet corner of the church, spectacles on nose, slowly reading his Bible, for he is a great student of the Scriptures. And he is never absent from session meetings, and regularly visits his district, for he is also an elder of the Church.

Now and then one has seen into the deep, emotional nature of the old man. The widows and the old feeble folk in his district know how tender his sympathy is. Many a time you may see him seated on the ground beside his broom, while the patiently gathered leaves waltz and whirl all over his path unheeded. For near him is some one of his people telling her story of anxiety or persecution, and he

An African Beadle

is so absorbed in his pastoral duties that he has forgotten his beadledom. After an hour or two has
passed, the missionary may expect a knock at his
office door, and the old man slowly enters, pushing
himself through the narrowest possible opening of
the door, and stands silently before he begins deliberately to unfold a story to which he has just now
been listening, and to ask advice about how the case
should be treated.

One day he came to my house and asked me to
let him hear how my machine sang, for I had recently brought out a little gramophone. I placed a
good record of the Hallelujah Chorus from " The
Messiah," and first explained to him the idea of the
music, of tier upon tier of angels singing the glory
of Christ, and translated the English words into his
own vernacular. Then I started the gramophone.
When the song began he was standing beside me
with curiosity written on his face. But after a little
I noticed that he sat down, and when the whole
glorious burst was over I turned to him to ask what
he thought of it. But his head was buried in his
hands, and he was silent.

At last I said, " Would you like to hear it again ? "
He looked up, and said, " No."

54

An African Beadle

Then I saw that he was weeping. Without a word of thanks, he turned and went off very slowly, leaving me more solemnized than I had ever been before by music, for I saw one to whom it had opened the gates of heaven, and who had been looking into glories ineffable.

IV

A HOLIDAY ON THE HILLS

FOR weeks the sun has been growing hotter and hotter. The dry land is stridently calling for rain with the voices of noisy crickets. But the trees which were standing bare and dead-looking for the past month have been putting forth buds which are bursting into soft leaves of most wonderful golden brown and crimson tints, and we know that up at our hill house the neighbouring woods will be a blaze of colour.

Here we move languidly. The schools have come to a close, the workers lose their energy by ten o'clock, and it is time that building and such-like work were being suitably finished off, for the rains are near. Indeed, the pale faces of the children, and the weariness of the parents, proclaim that the time for the little holiday has come.

So there is a pleasant bustle in the house to-day. The ox-cart has been drawn up to the door and is

THE ARTIFICIAL LAKE AT LOUDON

Formed by damming the valley of the stream. Below it lies the garden. The upper reaches give good drinking water for the villagers, and sanctuary for birds. The lower reaches give fine bathing for the boys and girls.

A Holiday on the Hills

now being loaded with bedding and boxes of clothes, pots and pails, and all the sundries that are necessary to family life in a holiday camp. Everything is well secured with reams of hide. Six oxen are yoked again, and with a crack of the long whip and an ear-splitting yell from the driver, the six patient beasts take on the strain, and slowly the loaded cart starts for the hill twenty-five miles off.

That night all go to bed early, finding sleeping quarters where they can, for we must start before dawn so as to arrive on the cool hills ere the midday sun has made travelling a purgatory. By three o'clock we are all awake and dressed, and after a breakfast by candlelight of warm tea and eggs, the expedition starts. The ladies and children leave first in bush cars and rickshaws, while I remain behind, waiting for the dawn, as I shall follow more rapidly on a motor-bicycle. They soon disappear in the dim starlight through the woods, but the sharp shouts of their runners, who pull their little machines, can be heard for long.

Two or three hours afterwards I mount my motor-bicycle and follow. Fourteen or fifteen miles out I make up on the convoy, steadily jogging on. The quick run has become a slow trot, for now the long,

A Holiday on the Hills

continuous climb has begun, and already the cool breezes from the " morning hill " fan us.

After a little rest, and a snack and a cup of tea, we start off again, and I run ahead to get the house ready for the arrival. Well up the hill I pass the cart, now on its last lap, and the patient oxen are straining at the yokes.

The final climb is very heavy, and the road is loose and broken. My engine gets furiously hot, and now and then, with a dig into the ground, one has to assist the machine to climb. At last we breast the hill, and run up to the little white-washed cottage that stands there so solitary.

The house boys have arrived before me, and already the rooms are swept, the old mats are laid, and the windows are open for the winds to blow through the rooms. A deep bath stands on the verandah full of clean cold water, and one has the drink of the year. Now there is but little left for me to do but wait for the arrival of the others, and that won't be for another couple of hours. So I throw myself on the ground, and bathe body and soul in the intoxicating air and scene.

Yesterday we were frizzling in the mid-winter heat, half-heartedly dragging ourselves through the

A Holiday on the Hills

long day's duties. Now up here the whole world is sparkling with the joy of life. We are at least five thousand feet above sea-level, on a tongue of the rolling grassy range that lies between us and Lake Nyasa. To the south, a thousand feet sheer below us, begins and stretches out the Chewa plateau, flat and wooded, broken in the hazy distance, forty and sixty miles away, by the great hills Kasungu and Ngara. In the clear mornings we will amuse ourselves by trying to catch the glint of the sun on the roofs of the Kasungu Mission Station, but I don't think we have yet been successful, even with our best glasses. In the near distance we trace the line of the river courses by the red earth of the village gardens. For it is only in recent years, since peace has come and war raids ceased, that this stretch of country has been repopulated, and the villagers always begin their fields near the rivers from which they draw their water. Here and there a little column of blue smoke is rising, marking the site of a village scarcely visible among the trees.

To the east there is a wild jumble of rocky kopjes and sudden hills, putting a barrier between us and the lake. Among the endless succession of deep valleys and steep hills there lives a scattered people,

A Holiday on the Hills

to whom Dr. Turner ministers. Once or twice he has suddenly appeared on our hill-top, breathless with his climbing, and only too happy to sit here for a day or two to breathe the quiet and vigour of the hills.

As the days pass, and the first rains fall and clear the air, misty with grass fires, we shall see the great lake gleaming in the morning sun like a piece of old silver plate, and rimmed by the low hills of Portuguese East Africa, a hundred miles away.

North and west the Ngoni plateau lies unbroken, reaching out into the blue mystery where land and sky seem to kiss each other. There lies the land of my heart, for as far as the eye can see, and far beyond to the west, live the people whom God has given me. A thousand villages sit invisible to the eye in that great plain, and more than a hundred schools. As I lie prone on the grass, with the cold winds around me, the silence of the world quietens me. The plain becomes a living soul with a throbbing personality, and the God of heaven and earth is spread over it. Little white, fleecy clouds flit through the sky far above me, slowly dissolving into invisibility. A hawk soars and dives with motionless wings through limpid space. But for the sigh of the life-giving breeze in the grasses there is no sound. The bright sun fills earth and sky with a glad light and warmth. Silence broods over us, and all around is God, through the quiet and the vastness speaking of glory and of love.

Presently little figures, no bigger than ants, can be discerned emerging from the trees and winding along the open slopes. Nearer and nearer they come, till gleams of white cloth amid the small black bodies reveal the Europeans. Faster and faster they move as they disappear over the last dip. When they next are seen, half an hour after, over the brow of the hill, panting and flushed, they are only a few yards from the house.

The most wonderful tea that ever was drunk is waiting them on the table, brewed in a great pot, for there is no stint to the number of cups the thirsty travellers will consume before they rise. Then there is an hour or two of bustle, putting aside into rough cupboards the table utensils, unpacking the boxes which came with the cart, hanging up the cloths, and little articles by which a lady transforms a barn into a pleasant dwelling-place, and by the afternoon all is ready for rest and ease.

A Holiday on the Hills

The quiet hill is alive with natives now. Some have come as carriers, others with provisions to sell, others in the hope of finding work, and all with the expectation of getting something to eat in the way of game. So I stroll out with my gun to some near little valley where I know game is likely to be found, and sit behind a rock. No living thing appears anywhere. But presently a tail is seen swishing among the trees, and then suddenly we become aware that two or three stately eland are quietly browsing near. We wait a little, and soon a great fat bull comes out into the open, cropping the short grass, and then two or three of his wives. They are quite at their ease, and stand still for long intervals looking into nothing. It seems a shame to shoot these quiet creatures, but the lust of hunting has seized me, and then there is the thought of the crowd of carriers and others, for whom this is going to be one of the great treats of the year. So I fire. It is an easy shot, and the great bull starts off with a speed of which you scarcely thought it capable, and you know that you need only follow a few yards over the hill and he will be found there stone dead. I hate the sight of a dying beast, and always think I shall never shoot again when I see the appeal of its black,

A Holiday on the Hills

pathetic eyes. Even when it is lying dead the sight is not pleasant. So I turn back to tell the people where the game is lying. Immediately the hill-top is deserted. Later at night the whole of the carcase is carried in, two men bending under the weight of a single leg. The meat is divided out, and with the first streak of dawn the followers have gone, loaded with flesh, to rejoice their hearts.

We soon fall into the normal ways of our holiday. The complete isolation is gone, unfortunately, but yet there is quiet rest.

The cottage is built on the top of a ridge. From our station, though it is twenty-five miles away, we can see it, a little black dot against the sky-line. It is a small three-roomed house built of sun-dried bricks and thatched with grass, and its erection cost us ten pounds. The floor is beaten mud, and the walls are washed with a creamy white clay that is found in abundance in the neighbourhood. Two small round huts for our servants stand alongside, and near by is a fenced cattle kraal for the milk cows we have brought with us. Half a mile off good clear water is found. From the house four rough roads run to the four points of the compass, each ending in a small outcrop of rocks commanding wonderful

A Holiday on the Hills

views. Among those rocks the children play all the day long ; little caves making magic mansions, and loose stones providing abundant material for further building extensions. Here the elders can sit for hours, with books in their hands, at times brooding over the deep wooded gorges that lie below, or the far-stretching plains, and now and then examining the grassy slopes with their glasses to see whether the game has yet come out into the open. As the afternoon advances they are sure to be rewarded.

Down below in the valley a dainty bush buck has stepped out from the cover in most ladylike fashion, her afternoon toilet completed, and is slowly moving into the grass, soon to be joined by her mate. Or, further off, a troop of zebra is advancing in single file, eating as they move, the white and black stripes shining in the sun. Down the hill-side four or five roan antelope are spread among the new green grass that is rapidly replacing the burnt patches. Then, as the sun comes near the horizon, a herd of eland appear suddenly from nowhere, a mighty bull leading, and twenty or thirty others, male and female, soberly moving like browsing cattle.

One day the servant girls and the children came

A Holiday on the Hills

home rapidly and full of excitement, for they had
seen a rhinoceros crossing the hill-side before them.
In the early days of our holidays on this hill, before
the game had been disturbed by our presence, the
beasts were very tame. We sat on a little ridge one
Sunday afternoon and saw a herd of at least thirty
eland slowly approach us. The children ran towards
them, but they only looked up and stared at the
little apparitions, and did not move away. It was
only when we all rose and ran towards them with
shouts that they turned at last, and trotted over the
edge of the hill.

In November or December, when the game come
out of the woods in search of the new grass that is
turning the open slopes to a pleasant green, our
camp is a hunter's paradise. Then, before sunrise
or towards sunset, we set off with our rifle and hunt
daily for an hour or two. The beasts do not swarm
in great herds as they do in some of the plains of
Africa, and make hunting more like massacring.
They are there mostly in threes or fives, and have
to be sought out and stalked carefully. But there is
variety to make the hunt constantly interesting. In
one holiday I have killed klipspring, bush buck, red
buck, gwape, zebra, roan, sable, eland, wart hog, and

A Holiday on the Hills

pig, and have seen, but not shot, jackal, hyena, and leopard, and heard the majestic roar of the lion somewhere in the neighbourhood.

When night falls we are all within doors, sitting over a supper table laden with the fruits of the garden sent up from the station—pineapples, strawberries, pawpaw, peaches, with cream that rises richly from the milk, for the feeding on the hills transforms the milk our cows produce, steaks from some great eland recently killed, or a tender roast from some of the smaller antelope, steaming Nyasaland coffee, never so fine as when cooked with the hill water, and drunk at the end of an exhausting hunt.

Then we sit round a blazing fire, while outside the wind sighs and rushes, making a noise round the gable of the house like the song of wind and waves about a great ship at sea.

When we look outside through the glass doors and windows, the great land is bathed in the softest moonlight, enchanting beyond words, and cold as an autumn day in Scotland. Mighty banks of mist sometimes gather about the highest ridges, and come rolling down, until the whole landscape is blotted out. We turn into bed with the music of

A Holiday on the Hills

a strong gale blowing about the house and the curtain of a sea of mist drawn tight about us.

So our days and nights pass, the heat forgotten, rivers of life flowing into us, while Africa lives through moods we knew well in Scotland, but scarcely expected to find here.

Now the great rain clouds are gathering day by day all over the vast horizon. Brilliant flashes of lightning and deep-rolling thunder proclaim that the rainy season is breaking. Here and there the clouds burst on the plain and bury sections of it in a black night of rain. Then one day they break on our hill-top. A deluge bars us in, as within guarded prison gates. It passes and frees us again. But the morning follows, covering us with blankets of white mist which are not withdrawn for hours. It is time we were back to the dry comforts of the station. Carriers are summoned from the near villages, and at dawn everything is put together, the house is locked up, and we run for the station from the damp, cold hill-top.

V

LOST IN THE BUSH

ON every side the ground spread out flat as a table, featureless, and without distinguishing marks to give the traveller natural sign-posts. Great mpani trees with scanty foliage covered the plain, growing close together, but affording poor shade when the scorching sun beat on the head of man and beast. For then the leaves close like a book, and hang vertically to escape the burning rays. The soil was baked with the heat, seamed by many cracks where water had lain in the wet season, and occasionally broken by a shallow, sandy river-bed now as dry as the caked surface of the plain, and blocked by bared roots or fallen dead trees. Occasionally there spread for miles a dry, hairy grass not many inches high which seemed to be dwarfed by a poisoned soil, and somehow had escaped the wide grass fires that had blackened all the rest of the plain. Near the path lay long strips of pure white ash, marking the place where a dry

Lost in the Bush

tree had smouldered in fire till nothing but ashes remained.

For miles we marched without seeing water. Indeed, our day's journey was largely planned by the distance of one water-hole from another. We started in the night if there was a good moon, or very early in the morning, so that we might pass through the thirsty distance before the sun became too hot. Ten or fifteen miles to the west of us ran a great river, the Loangwa, but its waters came from the hills far to the north, and from one or two tributaries which joined it on its western bank. On our side not one drop of water contributed to its flow, and the only sign we had of the neighbourhood of this river was when we drew nearer to its banks and met herds of waterbuck and other great game which frequent deeper and more abundant water than our infrequent pans afforded.

In the early morning before the sun rises, and while it is yet a cool blaze of light near the horizon, the wide woods are full of interesting life. Our eyes are all abroad, for at any moment we may spy a troop of zebra, or a quiet, browsing herd of eland, or two or three stately roan or sable antelopes. But when the sun shines in its strength all this mighty life of the plains disappears into the thickets and reeds where travellers cannot see them.

The woods, however, are never deserted. Herds of curious mpala are constantly flitting across the path and gathering in bunches of ten or twenty to watch us pass. Occasionally there is a clamour of quarrelling and barking, and then a great troop of baboons swings down from the trees and gallops clumsily away, until they sit on their haunches at a safe distance and bark at us. Myriads of gaudy little birds flash up and down with ever changing colours.

Through this most fascinating flat our path was running north and south, sometimes with a loose, sandy surface which carried the marks of the bare feet that tramped it; at other times faint or undiscernible to untrained eyes, for it ran over hard-baked soil on which the traveller's feet left no trace.

We had marched about four or five hours this morning when we came to our camping place beside a shallow water-pan. Round its edge the green grass grew in a belt some three or four yards deep.

Lost in the Bush

Out into the water there was more growth—grass, reeds, weeds, but all so refreshingly green that the eye rested and fed on it.

Here the men threw down their loads and stepped into the pond to drink. As the water was not fresh or inviting they stood and stooped to drink, throwing the water into the air with their hands, and catching mouthfuls.

My cook boy had marched at the head of the carriers and immediately started to collect dry wood. In a few minutes the pots were on a blazing fire, and porridge, eggs, and tea were being cooked for my breakfast.

While these preparations were going on I took up my rifle and wandered into the thicket which lay behind the water-hole to see whether I could find a buck for the men. Pushing through the dense bush, I came to an open space, blackened with a recent grass fire, and there sat down to look about me. The sun was in my eyes, and the wood beyond looked strangely dark. By and by I was conscious that there stood among the deep shadows an antelope. It was perfectly motionless, and all that could be seen was a head looking steadily at me with twisted horns above it. I quietly raised my rifle and fired.

Lost in the Bush

The bullet pierced its brain, and down the antelope fell.

As our resting-place was not far off I shouted, hoping that the sound of my rifle and perhaps my cry would bring up some of the carriers. After a little time had elapsed one lad appeared. He had heard the crack of the gun and, hoping that some animal had been killed, he had followed. I led him to the dead beast, then sent him back for the other men to skin and cut up the carcase, while I strolled slowly back to the camp.

By the time I arrived breakfast was ready and spread, and I sat down to eat in an agreeable solitude, for all the men had gone off to the kill. After breakfast I took up my gun and walked out into the wood, for I knew that a good hour or two would pass before the men returned with their loads of flesh.

The stroll was very quiet and pleasant. The sun was still low in the horizon. The trees cast their heavy shadows on the flat land, and there was no life visible except birds and little squirrels. I had no thought of hunting, and was using the leisurely hours to think out a problem of my work that interested me. So I wandered on, careless of the

Lost in the Bush

direction I was taking. Suddenly I became aware that a great bull eland was slowly moving among the trees a little way off. The opportunity was too tempting to be resisted. I began to stalk the animal carefully. By and by I fired, and hit him. But instead of dropping he went off at a steady trot, and I made after him. Again I got in a shot, but only made him run harder, and I, forgetful of distance and direction, ran in pursuit, dodging behind trees when there was any chance of his seeing me. At last we came to a dry river-bed, with its usual thicker growth. The eland tore across and disappeared among the leaves and branches. More quietly and carefully I followed, and when I emerged on the other side my game had disappeared, and I could not see where he had gone.

Somewhat disappointed with my loss, and not caring to go farther, I decided to turn back to camp, and so began to follow in what I fancied was the direction from which I had come.

I crossed one river-bed, and felt satisfied I was all right. But when I came to another a little farther on I was puzzled, for I only remembered having crossed one. Then I plunged into a thicket of dense growth, and I knew I had not been there

Lost in the Bush

before. However, I went steadily south, and yet failed to recognize any feature of the endless wood. Presently I saw a solitary waterbuck standing under a tree: only his head and horns were showing. Steadying my rifle against a branch, I fired at my small target, and the waterbuck fell stone dead.

Now I was puzzled as to how I should let my men know where to find the animal after I got back to camp, for I was hopelessly without sense of direction, and the wood all around was flat and without distinguishing marks. But, what was worst of all, I had no idea of the whereabouts of my camp.

So I decided to leave a little trace of my journey which would lead my carriers to the game and, at the same time, reveal to myself any possible returning on my path, for that, I knew, was the weakness of people lost in the wilderness. Now it had begun to strike me that I was lost.

Happily, I had a whole copy of the *Scotsman* with an account of the Assembly in my pocket. Tearing this into minute fragments, I dropped the flakes at intervals. They were easily discernible in the strong light lying on the bare, hard soil. For an hour I had been walking steadily when I came upon a wide pan of cracked mud where water had once stood. I climbed out of this little hollow, and lo! there were my paper flakes on the ground. Evidently I had completed my first circle! In utter consternation I sat down to think. At the same moment there was a rush, and I looked up in time to see a gnu and some reed buck tearing along near me. I let them go with no thought of shooting, for the problem that vexed me was how to get out of this trackless desert. At length I decided to move straight on east, for I knew that a native path ran north and south through the great valley, and, though its track was sometimes invisible where it ran along hard earth, much of it passed over a light, sandy soil. If I kept steadily going east I was bound to cross this path, if not to-day, then the next day.

So I started out, taking my bearings from the sun. Now and then I shouted, in the hope that perhaps my men were nearer than I thought, and all the time I kept dropping my little flakes of paper.

My shouts attracted a herd of mpala, which stood bunched together watching me. I could not resist the offer to shoot, so I fired, and one leapt into the air and dropped. I covered its body with leaves so as to hide it from the vultures, and then continued my march east. My mouth was parched with thirst, and I was growing extremely tired. As the conviction grew on me that I was lost I began to break into a run. Every now and then I had to sit down to prevent myself running, and to take stock of my general direction. The sun was now scorching hot, and the tenuous air rose in waves from the earth as from an oven. I poured out moisture from every pore, but neither water-pan nor water-bottle was near to slake my raging thirst.

I still continued to shout at intervals, but the curious result was that every time I called the mpala came leaping towards me. They gathered in big bunches of twenty or forty and watched me, and then followed in long strings near by me. As I had only one cartridge left I decided to keep it, in case I was benighted and had to use it for more dangerous game.

Utterly exhausted, I now sat down, and began to think what I should do if the night came on and I was still wandering. I looked about for a suitable

Lost in the Bush

tree to climb in which I could be safe, but none was visible there.

At last I got up again and resumed my weary tramp. The newspaper was finished by this time, and I had torn up all letters and papers with which my pockets had been well stuffed. At last I fell back on my diary, the only paper left me, and leaf by leaf I reduced it also to small flakes as I walked. Each leaf that fell was like the dropping of a treasure, for the little book was full of curious native words, travel notes, sketches of paths, and village locations. At last it too was finished, and nothing remained but its bare boards. I stood a moment to puzzle how I should continue to trace my track, for I knew that my faithful carriers must hit upon this utterly foreign thing, once they were alarmed at my absence, and following it must find me at last. Then suddenly I lifted my eyes and saw the path. There it was, running north and south over a slightly sandy soil.

That was one of the great moments of my life. No avenued and flowered road ever appeared so beautiful and dear as that little strip marked by the feet of human beings. There were the small cups in the sand where men's toes had trod, and the larger ovals of their heels. The deserted valley had suddenly passed from a gloomy solitude to a human habitation. Though man was not visible, were not these little marks evidence enough that he had passed this way, and that I was no longer alone among vast trees and companionless game? Men had passed along this way to home and friends, and so might I if I followed where they had gone.

But the greatest thought was the goodness of God, Who had led me at last to so plain a path just when my paper was finished, and where the feet of men could be seen.

I stooped down and examined the path very carefully. Soon it was evident that some steps were pointing north, while others had gone south. Now, where was my camp? North or south? The nearest village to the north was perhaps twenty miles away, but to the south it was further still. Had I passed this way in the morning? If I had, my camp lay to the south; if not, it was north. I scanned the sand most carefully to see if there was a straight ribbon mark of my bicycle wheel. But I could see none. Yet that was not decisive, for my bicycle was at the head of the caravan, and behind me at least fifteen porters had been tramping, and their feet may have obliterated the marks. So I walked north, watching the path very carefully. Sometimes no sign of the path was visible, for the earth was hard like wood. Then a wave of thankfulness would come that I had struck it at a sandy place, else I might have crossed it unawares.

I had not walked more than half a mile when suddenly I became aware of a little straight line appearing now and then on the path. Down I got on my hands and knees and examined this line. Yes, it was the spoor of something that had moved along that path. It must be the bicycle wheel. No other thing in a native caravan could leave this line.

So off I started south, at a great pace, and arrived back at the point where I had begun my walk north, just where the paper flakes had given out, and I raised another shout as I walked on rapidly. Immediately there came an answering call, and three or four natives broke through a screen of green shrubs and came running to me. I had actually hit on the path only a few yards from my camp.

The whole exploit was so foolish that I was ashamed to speak of it to the carriers who came running to welcome me. " Follow the line of little papers," I said, " and you will find some dead beasts I shot."

" Ah, sir, you are mocking us," they answered. " We were starting out to search for you."

" No, it is all true. First you will find a mpala, then, further on, a waterbuck. There is going to be a good moon, but you must hurry up."

Immediately there was a series of shouts, "*Nyama, nyama !*" (" Game, game ! "). And so the camp emptied, and everyone began to follow the scent at a trot like a pack of dogs. But I limped to my tent and threw myself on my bed, too tired to rise from it for hours afterwards. The blazing fires and my cook sitting over his pots gave me a glowing sense of companionship.

With the moon the men returned laden with their spoil. Dry logs were thrown on the merry fires, and far into the morning the men were busy cutting the flesh into long strips and spreading these over green-stick frames, where they frizzled and dried.

Next day as we tramped along, the men laden with dried meat on top of their bundles, one of them said to me : " But why did you drop the flakes of paper ? "

Lost in the Bush

" That you might find game," I said.

" It was a clever idea," he answered, unsatisfied.
" But you took a strangely winding way home."

And I, who have so little sense of direction, held
my silence before these men to whom no wilderness
or thicket hides the straight way home.

VI

"THE NEEDY ONE"

IN Africa cooking is peculiarly boy's work. Of course, when we speak of 'boys,' we put no limit on their age, and you may be surprised to find that the reputed "boy" is grey-haired perhaps, and a grandfather. Yet when the spirit of the people has seized you, you will not feel that there is any inconsistency in calling this veteran a boy. For does he not embody all the virtues of boyhood? In spite of his manly years he can run and dance, laugh in most boisterous fashion, and do the most absurdly irresponsible things. Until his decrepit body bows under the burden of years, and he goes softly with a sedate sobriety, he must always be a boy to the serious and restrained European.

Amid all the cooks who have passed through the apprenticeship of our kitchen, "The Needy One" left the most curiously mingled memories. That sad name, a tombstone to his dead father, was soon

" The Needy One "

left behind, and he took a high-sounding Biblical name more connected with wisdom and affluence than his former melancholy one. Yet he never forgot his lonely condition. This married family man could be heard sometimes remonstrating with small boys who would not collect the firewood he wanted for their treatment of him, an orphan.

" The Needy One " was a man of fitful temperament, occasionally capable of responding with strong emotion to higher appeals ; at other times so utterly careless and unreliable that the patience of his mistress broke and he was dismissed. Then he forgot all the restraint that the natural courtesy of the African imposed, and would leave in sullen indignation. He would fold his blanket with the little precious belongings—his mirror and razor, his white duck suit for Sunday wear, and a preposterous sun helmet. Carrying them he would go forth, his soft face clouded with dark passions. A few days would be sufficient to bring him back to his senses, and one morning he would be seen on the verandah, humbly suppliant, ashamed of his rudeness, and begging that he might come back to the sheltering moral atmosphere of the mission house. For he was a man of strong passions, and knew well that in the village it was not easy for him to live a straight life. His weak soul hungered for the family prayers and Christian bulwarks which gave him a safer passage.

One day he was reproved until his proud spirit rebelled and he said he was going home. His mistress told him he must now go for good, and could not be taken back. He went, thinking in his heart that he had chosen his time well, for a gathering of the Europeans was to take place within a week, and who could cook for the assembled guests ? Indeed, the next few days were anxious ones for the lady of the house as she tried to train another cook. But on the day before the visitors arrived " The Needy One " had installed himself in the kitchen, for, in cool reflection, his heart would not allow the *dona* to suffer this distress. From that day he never again threatened to leave so long as we remained in Africa.

It was in travel, however, that I tasted his unique qualities. He reckoned me a most precious and fragile trust which he had to bring back unbroken through the rough and tumble of bush adventure. At times his solicitous care was a terrible nuisance.

and was only bearable because it was so ridiculous.
More than once, when one was over-fatigued or in
bad health and his most tempting dish was put
aside untasted, I found him at the tent door in
silent tears. When I asked him sharply the meaning of this humbug, he would sob that I was not
eating, and he could not face my wife if he returned
me ill and famished to her care. Then there was
no remedy for his low spirits but that I should at
least make a pretence of eating what I had no
wish for.

It was a sight sometimes to see the arts by which
he gathered food for my table. No man could be
more wheedling and insistent with the old ladies and
the young girls of the village. He could find where
the eggs were when the people said there were none.
There was never a lack of girls to fetch the best
water in the neighbourhood for his cooking. Rows
of well-filled pots clustered about his fire while he
kept up a running chaff with the young bearers of
the water. No fatigue seemed to incapacitate his
power to cook. At the end of a long day's march,
while the men busied themselves erecting my tent
and laying out my belongings, he was preparing his
open fire with all the village children acting as

" The Needy One "

willing helpers. Then he squatted beside his primitive kitchen range, blinking in the smoke and attending to the four or five pots he had placed on the iron sheet set over the fire. If there was an omelette to prepare, he beat the eggs in a plate, dancing to the movement of the fork, while the children made an orchestra by clapping their hands and singing.

One day we were returning from the Loangwa Valley, where we had been travelling for weeks in a land where the tsetse fly rules and no cattle can live. All the time I had been without fresh milk— a very minor evil. But now we were up on the hills approaching the villages where the kraals were full of cattle. We had started off before the dawn, and intended to breakfast when we should come to the first village. We were not long on the march when I wanted to give some instructions to the cook, but " The Needy One " was nowhere to be found. The carriers were sure he had started in the dark along with us, but now he had disappeared. I feared some love imbroglio, for his heart was miserably susceptible. Yet we could do nothing but go on. About eight o'clock we were crossing an open glade, a mile or two from the first village, when the men cried

"The Needy One"

out, "'The Needy One'!" I looked and beheld, far along the glade, a herd of cattle rushing across, "The Needy One" at the tail, whistling, hulloing, and waving his clubs as he drove them along at full speed and disappeared into the wood behind them. Was this a cattle raid carried out in the spirit of the fathers?

When at last we arrived at the village the mystery was solved. For there at the kraal gate stood the patient cows lowing for their calves, while "The Needy One" squatted at the udder of one of them milking into one of my tins. Without leave or ceremony he had commandeered fresh milk for my porridge and proudly set the brimming vessel before me, a triumph of foresight and initiative.

We called him "Handy Andy" among ourselves, but there was something undignified about the sound of the name, and he resented it and would not adopt it, though we assured him it was a most euphonious English name.

Once I was travelling through the Marambo, where the sun burns fiercely and the tsetse bites with a persistence that no wariness can beat off. So we travelled at night. It was a dark, moonless night, and we moved very slowly through the open forest guided only by the feel of the narrow native path. " The Needy One " headed our line, and I was immediately behind, while the porters followed in Indian file. To give my cook confidence I asked him to take my shot-gun, and I put two cartridges into the barrels, while I carried my rifle. We had been marching for some hours, and were making a fair pace as the ground was flat and clear, and the path ran comparatively straight ahead of us. After a time I handed my rifle to a lad behind me. About two or three in the morning " The Needy One " suddenly stopped. There was a lion somewhere in front. The night was so dark he could not see it, but he declared that it was so near he could hear it breathing. Indeed, it seemed to be but a few feet away. He put his gun on the ground and searched his pockets for his cartridges, forgetting they were in the barrels of his gun. I turned to the lad behind me to get my rifle, but he was not there. He had fallen into the rear, confident that as we had proceeded so long without trouble I should not need my weapon. The lion gave a growl. The carriers behind us heard it, and raised at once a great shout of " Lion! Lion! " Then it seemed as if

A Native Blacksmith at Work under the Dove-cote
Grain-barns are seen in the distance.

Oxen Drawing a Cart on Loudon Station

the lion, hearing the sound of many and seeing none, thought flight its safest procedure. For with the shouting the beast crashed off through the bushes, and we neither saw nor heard it again. On the whole, I was glad that my blundering cook had forgotten about the cartridges, for had he fired he would have done more harm than good. All through the rest of the night he walked very alert, and when next a leopard called in the distance his gun was at his shoulder at once.

His anxiety to save me all inconvenience made him inventive beyond his practical sense, and sometimes caused more trouble than convenience. My motor-bicycle gave him much anxiety. One night he dreamed that he and I had gone up to heaven together. Next day he told my wife of the dream and insisted that she should get a bicycle for him, for he was sure that the motor-bicycle was to be my ladder to heaven, and he must be with me in the accident that would take me off. With me he urged that it was necessary that he should ride a bicycle when I also cycled, so that I should not have long waits at the halting places for my meals. At last I procured for him a solid-tyre bicycle, and then

" The Needy One "

when I ventured ahead I was closely followed by
my guardian angel. But it puzzled him to make
the situation easier. For he arrived with me ahead
of the whole caravan, while the food was carried
by men who walked, and though his bicycle was
there nothing else was there with which he might
cook.

It was delightful to see him flying along, careless
of the stumps and steep descents. One day I might
find him with the tyre all slipped off, loosened
with the great heat, while he was busy removing
the brakes and fastening the tyre with strips of
bark. Later on I might find him among the
stones at the bottom of a hill, his wheel buckled
and his face and hands smeared with earth and
blood.

In one of my numerous journeys we were nearing
home when heavy rain met us. About four miles
from the station we came to a swollen river which
was rushing with some violence and seemed impass-
able. It was provoking to be held up so near home,
and it looked as if we had no alternative but to spend
the night there and wait for the river to go down.
But my eager cook took a long rope we had with us
and tied himself to the end of it. Several men held

it tight, and he entered the river with another lad. It was not too deep to prevent them from walking and breasting the current, but they had to cross in a long slant, and were only saved from being carried away by the pull on the rope. Twice or thrice they lost their footing and were hauled back to the firm bank. At last they got across and tied the rope to a tree on the other side. Then I attempted the torrent, holding on to the line, and going across hand over hand. The stream was so strong that my body was stretched out on the surface of the water, but the assisted passage was made easy and safe. We then shouted our farewells to the carriers, who went off to sleep in some villages further down the river, and we tramped on to the station.

A mile from home we came to another stream deep but quiet. " The Needy One " stepped into the water without removing his clothes, for he had always a curious sense of the respect due by the cook to his master. I protested that the river was deeper than he fancied, but he was sure that it was quite shallow and would not reach beyond his hips. I mounted on his shoulders, and he started confidently to carry me to the other side. But he had scarcely

taken more than two or three steps when he plunged
up to his neck. With great difficulty I kept my
balance while he slithered across, keeping his head
well up and gripping my legs like a vice, until he
brought me safe to the other side.

My wife's trials, however, were of a more dis-
tressing kind. Once she had prepared a nice jelly
for dinner when we had some passing travellers
staying with us. She left it in a cool place, greatly
pleased with her triumph. When the time to eat it
arrived, there was no jelly there. "The Needy One"
had placed it in the oven to keep it nice and warm
for the table, for had not the *dona* tried so patiently
to teach him that we liked our food served up
hot ?

The simple needs of a mere man out in the bush
presented no such difficulties. The only problem
was to prevent the cook from being demoralized by
a month's continual movement. But his instructions about cleanliness were so emphatic that the
last day out was a very strenuous one for him. Then
he gathered his little satellites and made them scrub
dirty pots till they shone, while he carefully over-
hauled every spoon and plate, so that he returned
to civilization with an immaculate equipment which

" The Needy One "

assured my wife that every care had been expended in making things clean and sweet. But had she dropped in among us when we were still in the midst of our journeys that would have been another story.

VII

THE MOTOR FIEND

AFRICA is a leisurely land, unaccustomed to the haste and bustle of motor and steam locomotion. But no hoary tradition or sense of the fitness of things can deliver it from the intrusion of hurry. Lions have taken possession of railway stations, and leapt through the windows of a standing railway carriage, but the soulless booking clerk still sits at the office window issuing tickets, and trains still cross the bush and wide veldt spaces. Motor-cars run where weary slave caravans trudged their hopeless march, and motor-bicycles race bewildered antelope.

In our land a generation ago there appeared a mighty wonder of human ingenuity. The old chief who led the invading army of marauders sat on an ox, for he was lame, and this stolid creature went with its precious burden where its rider willed. Then those superhuman folk, the white men, appeared, and it was reported that some rode on horses. "What kind of animal is a horse?" I heard one man ask the story-teller.

"It is a great beast as large as an elephant, with a long tail like a gnu's, that sweeps along the ground ; and its speed is awful, no man or cow could race it."

"Ah these white men ! God has not made us like them. They say that they play with lions and can make the zebra carry them."

But when the motor-bicycle came it excited no admiration for the man who devised, or rode it. It was simply a magical marvel to be accepted like the lightning. A penny mechanical crocodile which I set down in the midst of a circle of chiefs was a vaster wonder than the bicycle. They ran from it, and roared with laughter, and danced about it, and the fun and genius of it never ceased.

There is a flavour about pioneering which can never be found by those who follow the beaten track, and I tasted it as deeply as man could the first day I rode a motor-bicycle along the roads of Ngoniland. For not only the people themselves, but I also saw it for the first time. Some one had told me there was a little F.N. motor for sale in the colony, and I, who walked hundreds of miles every year in my wide parish, thought this would double

The Motor Fiend

my powers. So I bought it and asked that it should be sent up to our hill country.

One day when I was returning from a six weeks' tramp in the far west, I heard that it was at the Government station awaiting me; so, with the eagerness of a boy for a new plaything, I made straight for the station. There stood my giant toy, and the magistrate and I circled round it trying to find out how it worked. He had read about motor-bicycles, and could name the parts, but was not sure of their identity. At last we filled up with petrol and oil. I mounted and pulled some levers. He and the native police shoved off, and lo, away went the machine with a splutter and a volley. I waved my good-byes, and headed for home, twenty miles away. A little experimenting with the levers revealed how the pace was regulated. But my hope was that the machine would not stop on the way, for I knew not the mystery of starting it alone, and then I hoped that when I arrived I should be able to stop and dismount with safety. It was a wildly exciting journey, but all my hopes were realized.

The first experiment was so successful that I determined to make a longer journey to Living-

The Motor Fiend

stonia, 140 miles away. A road was being made by Government, a simple track with the tree stumps cleared and the grass scraped from the surface of the ground. The numerous little river dips were being bridged in simple fashion with branches overlaid with clods of earth. Already about one hundred miles had been completed, so my carriers and tent were sent on to await me at the road end, while I should follow in four or five days. Off went the carriers, telling me I was foolhardy, and warning me that lions were terrorizing the villages near the road end. During the next few days I busied myself with station affairs and played with the motor-bicycle till I understood its ways better.

Then one bright morning I rose at dawn and, leaving my wife somewhat uneasy about my journey, started off. I passed through the Government station to the excitement of magistrate, police and prisoners, who all gathered to watch my rapid progress. Ten miles farther on I saw a family party leisurely filling the road with their bundles. I sounded my horn. Consternation seized them. They dropped their loads, and fled for their lives into the bush, and I swerved to avoid collision with their impedimenta. This made my bicycle touch the bank and it stopped. I got off, and tried to make it go again, but all power had fled, and it was dead. I unscrewed nuts, examined what parts I could look at, but nothing abnormal appeared. Dirty, thirsty and disgusted, I wheeled my machine back ten miles to the Government station. For hours the magistrate and all his assistants worked with me trying to find the mystery of the stoppage but nothing would induce the machine to respond to our efforts. At length at one o'clock we turned into bed. I lay in bed wide awake and reviewing our overhaul of the machine. Then suddenly it struck me that the points of the magneto were not adjusted, and with that I fell asleep. Next morning when I got up I went straight to the machine, and in ten seconds it was going again. There is no music so sweet to the distressed motorist as the regular sound of the explosions after a puzzling stoppage.

After breakfast I started again, and made good speed. Thereby another novelty of motor-bicycles was revealed. They have an unexpected faculty of shaking loose the articles tied to the carrier. Somewhere on these long stretches I dropped my lunch, then my tea kettle, then my sweater, till

The Motor Fiend

my carrier was bare. The road was very long, for heavy sand in the dry bed of a river is a tedious obstacle. The hills, too, were very stiff, and the engine very light, so I had to push up many a long hill, while the sun beat upon me and melted me. At last the sun went down when I was still twenty miles from the road end. The night soon closed about me, but a fine full moon was shining and gave sufficient light. I was now in the lion-infested land, so I proceeded with as much noise as could be produced by engine and horn. The dips to the river beds became very frequent and severe. My engine could only carry me up the steep gradient on the other side if I came tearing down at full speed. The difficulty was that I was never sure that there was a bridge at the bottom of the dip, but I must chance it and rush down so that I could climb again. I approached one stream, throttle open, horn going, and all the din possible accompanying me lest a lion might be waiting round the corner, when suddenly I came on two belated native travellers. They had heard the noise and I saw them draw up at the side of the road, raise their shields and poise their spears waiting for the coming of the awful monster whose strange sounds had alarmed them. As I flashed past they fell among the bushes in sheer horror, dropping spears and shield, and I disappeared into the dark.

At last the road ended. I blew blasts on my horn and my carriers appeared. A search party was out seeking for the lost master who had so rashly attempted the impossible. And that night the camp fire rang with stories of the wonder of the European, and with this, his latest madness.

A month after, a native brought to my wife a little package he had picked up on the road. She gave him a shilling for his honesty and opened the bundle. It was my lunch—mouldy bread, rotten bananas. But where were the kettle and the sweater and other returnable articles?

For a long time two little white boys played a game which was called after me. The older boy rode his little tricycle and dropped articles on the road; his younger brother picked them up and hid them. That was their impression of what my trial trip was like.

VIII

THE AFTERMATH

WE had all settled down nicely after the Great War had finished : men were home after long absence, and were busy rebuilding or repairing their houses. Round the evening fires the most wonderful tales tumbled and ran like a Highland burn in spate. The old men sat open-eyed when the younger ones told of " flying birds," with white men on them, which disappeared across the clouds. New words were coined for the machine-gun, and onomatopæic syllables described with awful vividness the rattle of the gun and the swathes of dead that marked its sweep. Roars of laughter followed the comical tales of queer situations, of terror-bound porters and the absurd attempts of white officers to make their commands intelligible.

There was more money in the land than ever had been there before, and young men were wandering here and there, trying to pick up cattle

The Aftermath

as dowry for their wives; and others, filled with visions of a great trading practice, were hawking calico, in which they had invested their savings. Life seemed easy and rich after years of forced labour in which thousands had laid down their lives. And though no medals had been struck, and no honours had appeared in the gazette for those porters who had done so much to win the war, the relatives of the deceased had become unexpectedly rich by the liberal grants of the Government. Suddenly through this cleared atmosphere rumour flew, like a bird of evil omen, carrying tales of terrible sickness and death that were spreading through Africa.

We heard of waggon loads of corpses being buried in great pits, of villages wiped out, of mine compounds which had been swept clean of labourers. Of course there was much exaggeration in Dame Rumour's tales, for she selects only the most likely to make your flesh creep. But some telegrams and the printed newspaper confirmed our fear. Influenza was swinging through the Continent like a gigantic scythe.

Now it was no hard matter to isolate Nyasaland, and the Government quickly took precautions,

The Aftermath

trying to close the paths of communication. But one day there crossed the wild stormy lake a canoe full of natives from Portuguese Africa. When they arrived on the British coast at some secluded spot, each passenger had to be lifted ashore, for influenza had seized them on the way. And thus the hospitable people lifted from the canoes and brought within their homes the carriers of the deadly scourge.

Soon it was raging everywhere. But before it broke out we had time to organize some help. In each village orderlies were appointed whose duty it was to visit all the sick when 'flu came, to see that they had firewood and water, and that food was cooked for them. Medicines were distributed among the leading teachers, which they were to give to the sick. All public gatherings of any sort ceased.

By these precautions we were able to diminish somewhat the severity of the disease, and possibly thousands of lives were saved. Yet there was no checking its progress. Not a village escaped, and in our tribe over two thousand died. Many of those who had been very ill lost their mental balance. The sickness found the weakest point in the neurotic African, and attacked his brain. Some wandered about in the bush, mad and restless, and for healing they sought out the witch-doctors. The treatment they received gave some of them power to become witch-doctors in turn, and thus these charlatans multiplied exceedingly, till they held in thrall this land in which schools stand in almost every group of villages for dispelling ignorance and superstition by the giving of wisdom. Every night you could hear the rattle of their drums in this direction and in that. Sometimes above the exciting insistence of the drums you might hear the distant sound of the chorus the villagers sang, and the nerve racking He! He! of the wizard's yell.

It was irritating enough to have this nightly activity going on for hours, making sleep impossible, but there were deep dangers. The sorcerers were " smelling out " here and there the magical causes of the influenza epidemic, and ventured to point out this man or that woman as having brought all the sickness and death upon their community. Sometimes the protests of the innocent compelled the administration of the poison ordeal, sometimes the accusation put the victim in peril of his life, and

The Aftermath

always it led to fierce quarrels and the final breaking up of villages.

Many a time I met these " Witch-doctors " and " Chiefs of the underworld " on the path or in the village, sometimes in full war paint, at other times concealing every trace of their criminal practices. Once or twice I induced them, by bluff, to hand over their drums, and dresses, and instruments, but never, I fear, by the persuasion of reason.

Meanwhile the magistrate was much concerned with the unrestrained growth of this disturbing evil. But he found it almost impossible to get a conviction against any one. No chief and no villager dare make an accusation, lest the sorcerer turn his magic upon them, for faith in magic has struck its roots deep into African soil. At length we agreed that the church must take action. So we got the magistrate's approval to our plan of campaign, and made sure that one of the big chiefs, who is a Christian, would back us up energetically.

One Sunday, when there was a fairly influential audience present, I preached a sermon against witchcraft. The severity of the Levitical law, with the death penalty, was expounded. Then clause by clause the gazetted law of the Protectorate was read and emphasized, no small stress being laid on the long years of imprisonment to which the criminal was liable, and slowly and with reiteration the clause was translated which makes a chief and a headman liable if he knowingly allows the poison ordeal and such like customs within his sphere. It was announced that the Government was keen to prosecute, and already five witch-doctors were under arrest. Then we said that a time of grace would be allowed, until the 8th of May. All witch-doctors who renounced their work before that, and registered their renunciation, would not be prosecuted, but after that date all who practised the art would be liable to immediate prosecution and severe penalties.

On Monday I made a hundred copies of a summary of all this, and a free translation of the law, and sending them to all the schools, asked the teachers to read them to the chiefs and head men, and to urge them to take action at once. For two days we waited, wondering whether our big policy of bluff was going to end in success or in failure. On the evening of the third day a weird procession marched up the avenue to our house. In the failing light they seemed fierce and awful. They were a company of witch-doctors and chiefs of the under-world. Their heads were dressed in hideous bunches of feathers and bladders, their loins surrounded with a fringe of cats' tails and curled hide. Carrying their drums and their bags of implements in their hands, they laid everything at my feet, and declared their purpose of abandoning for ever their unholy calling.

I read to them solemnly the law against witch-craft, and when they had been duly impressed I took their names, and sent them on another day's journey to the magistrate, that they might also renounce before him, and be registered. From that day they began to flow in. The headmen, finding that they also were in danger should it be proved that they had allowed certain practices to be carried on, began to sweep up all the known sorcerers in their district. This was done from no high motives of justice and progress, but from personal dread that they might suffer also. I have a theory that no chief or ruler among us ever acts from a sense of duty to the state, but from pressure brought by self-interest or other parties, and all his most energetic service is given when his person or property is threatened.

The Aftermath

At intervals all through the day the miserable half insane creatures were arriving. Again and again I went out to read the law, and to register their renunciation. Their accoutrements were laid at my feet. Gradually I was becoming acquainted with all the ugly paraphernalia that make up a witch-doctor's outfit. The drums we all know, their ear-splitting din in the night keeps us all awake. The head-dress and bladders and loin tags, a filthy vermin haunted mass were there too. Then I would ask for the zebra tail used in smelling out, or the walnut shells for divining, the beads, sticks, carved or plain, which turned and pointed to the accused. The bags of roots and medicines which were administered to the patients, or thrown into the wells to bewitch a village. As these were turned out, scores of small cockroaches went scurrying away, like evil spirits afraid of the light, and the men beside me started off in vigorous pursuit lest the loathsome creatures should propagate and fill my office with their breed.

Sometimes a witch-doctor would hold back some stage property that he valued. We would demand this also, and refused to register him until he returned with them. Then the beadle carried all

The Aftermath

the stuff to the church and laid it before the
communion table, until the platform was blocked
with drums, skins, dresses, medicines, bags of shells
and walnuts, and all the vile accumulation of the
sorcerer's art.

Miserable, wild, half-insane creatures most of
these penitents were. Some had not practised the
art for twenty years, but their chief had hounded
them out, and compelled them to gather their
rotting treasures and bring them to me. Others
were novices whose mental balance had been upset
by the influenza. And some gave us painful
surprises.

A poor naked woman with a sad worn face sat on
the verandah beside her basket of implements. Her
hair, grown long with neglect, was sticking out
from her head in a wild tangle, giving her a most
bestial and fierce appearance.

" What is your name ? " I asked.

" Jeannie," she said.

The name startled me, for it was not the usual
old native name which carried the stamp of
ignorance. An English name showed that she had
once been at school, perhaps had been baptised.
I looked at her carefully, and gradually gathered

some features that reminded me of a sweet-faced girl whom I had baptised years ago.

" What ! Jeannie, have you, too, become one of the servants of darkness ? "

" I have been ill and mad," she said with a sad voice, her head bowed with shame. " I lived in the bush away from people, and the witch-doctor cured me, and gave me his power to practise his art."

" He did not cure you. He has made you an enemy of God and of your own people."

" O sister, repent," the old beadle cried, with infinite sorrow in his voice. " There's still mercy for you."

But she only hung her head lower, the apotheosis of despair.

" Do you renounce your witchcraft ? "

" Yes, there are all my implements," and she passed them to me.

Then the old beadle spoke again, with a tear in his voice, reminding her of the power of God she once knew.

The most famous witch-doctor in all the land appeared, along with a dozen others, most of whom had been his disciples. His body was all scarred with self-inflicted wounds, for in the frenzy of his dance he was wont to beat himself with a club till the blood was streaming from him.

" Hullo, old friend," I cried, " have you, too, been hunted out ? "

" I have not practised since the war began," he said.

" Well, you did as much evil before the war as a regiment of witch-doctors. How did you come to give up practice ? "

" I was imprisoned, and told that I would get a long sentence if I was found out again."

" Well, your sentence will be longer even than that if you practise now," I added sternly. " Do you renounce for ever ? "

" Yes," he cried, and I registered.

" But, sir, I am a doctor now," he volunteered, when I had written his name. " Am I allowed to practise my profession ? "

" What is your speciality ? " I asked.

" I make queen cows to calve, and barren women bear children. My medicine has mighty power."

"You have only changed the lines of your deception," I said.

" No, sir, my medicine is genuine. Ask so and

The Aftermath

so, and so and so, if their wives have not borne children since they drank my medicine. I have engagements to go to the Chewa tribe, and to the Chipeta, and my reputation is all over the land."

"You old trickster, you are still too wise for a credulous people, but there is no law against your skill."

The vast heap of charms grew about our communion table. Visitors were dropping into the church all day to look at the strange collection. The terror of their implements seemed to have been dispersed. And now the people handled them, and laughed over them, and told stories of what this thing and that other thing had done, and how silly the poor deceived folk had been.

At last when the 8th of May arrived, we found that one hundred and fifty-two medicine men had registered, and made public renunciation. The land had been swept clean of the terror that had held it, and once more the wizards had disappeared. Next day all the mess was gathered together in one great heap and the beadle applied a match to the lower tier, and soon the whole was a blazing, smelling mass. But not until a few of the more interesting implements had been collected and saved

The Aftermath

from the fire for the benefit of one or two European curio hunters, who could handle the ugly and crude instruments with no fear, and with some wonder as to how such things as these could inspire wonder and fear in the minds of a simple people.

IX

A TRUE KNIGHT

WE were passing through the commercial
capital of Nyasaland, a gem set in a
ring of hills, when we first met Hammerton. A high official had invited us to dinner,
and we had gone forth, with lanterns in our hands
to lighten our way and to reveal any snakes that
might be lying on our path. We were all dressed,
out of respect to the Government, and its high
official who had honoured us with an invitation.
But that night we would fold away our starched
things and dress clothes, for next day we were to
start for the far interior, and it was the common
report that when we missionaries breast the hill
where we have our last look at the capital, we take
off our collars, and never wear them again until
that day, five years afterwards, when the embryo
city again begins to appear.

Two or three minutes before the dinner hour we
arrived at the house on the top of a hill where the

A True Knight

official was wont to bury himself in great volumes of history and law, far from the disturbing sounds of the busy town, the shouts and songs of the *machila* carriers, and the crack of the waggon driver's whip. But our host was not at home. This did not disturb us much, and with a chuckle we said we would come in and wait. For we knew that the official's hospitality was so generous that his memory sometimes failed to keep pace with it, and he had the great disadvantage of being a bachelor.

After sitting for some time among his books, our host burst in among us with many apologies. He had met five Government and Military Officers just arrived off the train, and had invited them to dinner, so we must wait a little until they had arrived. This was fortunate for us, for now we knew that this invitation had been so recent that the cook was bound to know that a dinner must be served, and as we afterwards learned house boys were at that moment hurrying to the nearest houses, borrowing fowls and vegetables and tinned fruits.

By and by the officers arrived. They were all young men, some civil, some military. And they were as stiff and shy as school-boys suddenly dropped at a dinner table of foreigners. Among them was

A True Knight

Hammerton, a fair-haired, clean shaven youth, with the figure of Apollo, and a shy smile that just suited the blushes that spread over his face when he was addressed by any of us.

At an hour when respectable Africans are preparing to turn in for the night, dinner was at last served, with all the abundance and variety that a hospitable bachelor seems always able to conjure up from nowhere and nothing in this land of magic. In our innocence we knew nothing of the scurry of unreadiness that had happened in the back premises, and of the feverish messengers who had returned from successful errands. We believed that in the high life of Government Officialdom it was the usual thing to dine when others go to bed.

That night Hammerton was quiet, for he was quite new to the country, and was overshadowed by men much his seniors, who spoke a language he scarcely understood about things and events which were far beyond his world. Yet he came with a name that was already famous to all who delight in Rugby football. The papers all knew his name, for few 'varsity men had ever attained to such perfection as he had. He had also taken a good degree, for exams carried no terrors for him. Yet

A True Knight

with a strange inability to use his powers to any practical end, he had already been the plaything of fate, and had travelled round the world, in strange situations.

First he had tried his luck in Australia, opening a practice, expecting that his law degree and honours in the schools would roll up clients to his door. But no one seemed to know him, and his capital gradually dwindled to nothing. His sporting spirit would not allow him to tell his people of his failure to amass a fortune, or ask for any relief. So he started out to cross the world without a penny in his pockets. He easily found a berth as a stoker in a mission steamer, and thus he cruised among the garden islands of the Pacific, and helped to carry missionaries from one island to another.

There was something strange about this young athlete that made him feel more at home among the rough stokers than among his equals, who like himself had been bred in luxury, and had taken honours in the Oxford Schools.

When he landed in California he found himself up against the emigration officers, for he had no capital in his pocket to satisfy their conditions, and no trade to which he had been apprenticed. But

A True Knight

he saw an open door before him when he described his occupation with humorous truthfulness as a " Brass finisher."

Now he had come among us to open a new career as an official of the Government, and certainly, if ever a man seemed certified to rise, this man with the powers of body and mind that were his had his foot upon the ladder. But through all the years that he lived among us, he shrank from any task that carried responsibility, or called for judgment, and so he kicked the ladder from him every time he had the opportunity to climb.

Yet no one could accuse him of mental indolence. The Government offers money grants to those who pass certain language tests, and law exams, so as to increase the efficiency of its servants. Hammerton sat for his law exam., and passed without an effort. He tackled each language of the Colony in succession, and passed, and then he learned Portuguese, spending part of a furlough in Lisbon to perfect his accent. Yet even this did not give him the station on the Portuguese border on which he had set his heart.

I remember meeting him one evening just after he had this last rebuff. He had strolled along to

A True Knight

the rest house where I was spending the evening, which happened to be not far from his official residence. The years had made little difference to his appearance. He wore a white shirt open at the neck and rolled up to the elbows, displaying a pair of magnificently developed arms. He wore shorts, very short, and socks, with his feet encased in cheap rope-soled shoes. In his mouth there hung a pipe, in which he smoked endlessly the vilest black shag. For the hour or two he sat with us he groused all the time against his superiors with a quiet humour that took all sting and bitterness from his grousing.

There was not one item of respect in his mind for the great officials to whom he was subordinate. And when he detailed his last interview with the powers, at which he had reminded them of a half promise to be sent to his desired border station, and had been rebuffed, he set us into fits of laughter as he drawled out the amazingly indiscreet and disrespectful remarks he had addressed to his High Mightiness. How he was not dismissed the service at once was a wonder, but how he was never advanced a step further was not.

Money seemed to have no value for him. His official income was small enough in all conscience, but it must have taken a considerable private income to meet his annual expenses. Yet he lived in utter simplicity, content if he had a chair to sit on, a table from which to eat his food, and a bed of any sort to lie on at night. A little bowl stood on the mantelpiece into which he put a supply of gold. His cook boy helped himself to this when he needed to buy food for his master's table, and reported when it was empty that he might replenish it. When he left for home on furlough he distributed his household goods among his boys, a bicycle to the cook, a sewing machine to his table boy—what in the world did he do with a sewing machine ? No wonder that his household staff found it difficult to get employment in any well-organized household when he went on leave.

I fancy that no man ever before came to the Colony with so beautiful and well developed a body as Hammerton had. To see him at his vigorous exercises in the morning would be the joy of any artist. And every morning, in the cold of the hill station, a strange figure, clothed in pyjamas only, could be seen racing down from his house to the chilly mountain river that flowed half a mile away, and plunging into a deep pool for his daily dip.

MISS HAVEL WITH HER SEWING CLASS OF WOMEN AND GIRLS IN A VILLAGE.

Note the huge bundles of grass which the women have carried in on their heads for thatching the houses. The women sit in characteristic attitudes. Chairs are unpopular with them.

A True Knight

When he was stationed at the lake shore, he could be seen almost every week striding from his lonely station along the lake shore, devoid of shoes or stockings, taking a twenty or thirty mile constitutional, which generally ended in the mission doctor's house, where he loved to visit and, sitting with his bare feet, drink cup after cup of strong tea.

These lonely walks gave many an anxious hour to his senior magistrate when he happened to be stationed with a companion. For he walked out alone, without gun or stick, or any weapon, and often did not return till long after dark. One night, on his return, he told with entire nonchalance that he had met a leopard on the path, and had attacked it with his fists, and driven it away before he continued on his journey. The story would be absolutely incredible but for the fact that he never boasted, and let fall the most wonderful adventures as if they had been commonplace occurrences.

I think he could have no enemies, unless it was among the hide-bound officials, who could not understand him, and who were constantly irritated by his refusal to accept responsibility. Though one day, by some strange freak, he rose to great heights, and showed himself a mighty lawyer.

A True Knight

For when he was stationed at the point where the one railway system enters British Territory, he found some flaw in the customs arrangements, and arrested the train. The engine might snort its most strident indignation, the guard storm and tear his hair, the impatient passengers swear and rage. But Hammerton put the whole caboodle under arrest, and dared them to defy his authority. A great case arose over this which had to go eventually to the High Court, and the Government lost its case, though there are lawyers who believe that Hammerton was in the right all through. It certainly gave him vast amusement, for he smoked his black shag, and quietly chuckled over all the bother he had raised, and the reams of correspondence, and hundreds of pounds the high and mightinesses had to pay out. But though his chances of favour and advance were now for ever blotted out, he only groused in good humour about the whole administration crowd.

But few knew that this gallant knight, who knew no respect for authorities, and had no sense of discipline, wrote to headquarters when he found that the action had gone against them, and earnestly and sincerely offered to pay the whole costs of the proceedings. One of his fellow-magistrates has said to me, " He had the barbaric virtues almost to excess, and was true to ' the salt he ate.' He should have been one of Malory's knights, not called upon to decide nice points or to judge and condemn ' his brother,' but merely to put down his head, and go for his king's enemy wherever met, and to succour distressed damosels—how shyly and chivalrously he would have done it ! "

But even a first-class constitution like his could not defy for ever the abuse that carelessness and exposure gave it, and his eyesight began to fail him. This was the time for him, in his strange contrari-ness, to be captured by the thrilling zest of elephant hunting. No sense of danger, and no lack of vision, interfered in the slightest with his zeal for hunting. The mission doctor, who loved him greatly, warned him more than once that his habits of life must change, and that so dangerous sport was not for him. But he only laughed at his fatherly warnings.

At last the end came, under most tragic circum-stances. He had a friend staying with him at his little station. One morning he went out early with some natives to burn the grass near at hand, so that hunting might be easier for himself and his friend. He was busy spreading the fire among the tall dry grass, which was roaring and crackling like a battery of maxim guns, when suddenly a rhinoceros charged him from the cover of the grass. He was too blind to see it coming. The sound of its rush was drowned by the noise of the grass fires, and he was caught by its formidable horn, skewered through the stomach and tossed. He rose when it passed, and undoing his puttees, tied up his wound from which the bowels had been protruding. Then with an almost incredible effort he walked back to his station. His friend immediately procured a *machila*, and laid Hammerton in it, and set off for the nearest doctor, who was fifty miles away.

What the pain and agony of that journey was no one can say, yet not a groan had escaped from him. The only word he spoke was when he said to his friend, " I hope no Germans are suffering as I am."

Yet he had offered again and again to go to the war and fight. One would have thought that officialdom would have been glad to have got rid of him in so honourable a way. But it was contrary to regulations, and when he threatened to desert the service that he might enlist, the severest penalties were held over him.

A True Knight

At length the mission station was reached. Hammerton was still alive. An operation was attempted, but he passed away before it could be completed.

To-day we all speak of Hammerton with love and reverence, for no one could meet him without being captured by the great beauty of his body, and the modest selfless man who seemed capable of doing almost anything but carry responsibility, or build an edifice for himself in which he could comfortably live.

X

A WANDERER RETURNED

MATEYU is a stalwart lad, one of the best teachers I have known. He has not had much education, but he had a natural gift for teaching that made him a treasure. Long before the school bell rang at seven o'clock he used to start off for the nearest villages to hunt up his pupils, and when the bell was still ringing out its prolonged appeal, he would march into the station at the back of a long file of merry children, as good humoured as himself, though he had compelled them by his own peculiar arts to come to school, and leave their fascinating play.

In school he taught with a merry twinkle in his eye, and many subtle tricks which kept his pupils alert. " O " was an egg, " e " a little house with a door, and two little rooms, " i " was a small boy with a hat, " u " was a little pot, " t " a fish-hook, " m " a man with three legs, and so on through all the alphabet, till each was a picture not foreign at all, but reminiscent of their own village life.

One thing that kept Mateyu full of fun and good humour was his sweet-faced wife, Ellen, with whom he was deeply in love. She thought no end of the genius of her husband, for he was head of a village, and kept the neatest of round huts, and the tidiest village in all these parts, and was the priest of the people.

Yet all his valued service, and home affection, could not restrain the spirit of adventure that seized him, when he listened to the stories of other lads who had wandered far afield in search of gold and new experiences in lands which seemed to be at the other end of the earth. At last he asked to be let loose from school work, that he too might seek his fortune. With great reluctance I let him go, and commended him to a friendly trader who had opened stores in far North-west Rhodesia. Then Mateyu bade farewell to wife and children, and with his food packed into a great goat-skin, and borne upon his shoulders, he stepped out for the lands of his dreams.

At first he was a good correspondent, and letters came from him regularly, full of messages for his old friends, and stories of his new experiences. His wife, too, was well supplied with money, and loving letters. Then he tired of his master, and started forth for the gold-fields to earn larger money there.

The years passed, and we did not lose sight of him. Now and then returning labourers brought word of him and presents of money for his family. Sometimes a cheque from the British Vice-Consul in the distant land in which he worked found its way to me, with a letter from Mateyu telling me to keep the money for him against his return. And so his account grew, until I had more money in trust for him than a poor teacher could save in several lifetimes. Each letter was full of his old optimism and force, but there was no word of his return.

At last all communication ceased. The years passed and we could get no word of our wanderer. One day his eldest son came to me, a big burly youth, the very image of his father, and said that he had now reached man's estate, would I let him have some of his father's money to pay dowry for a wife, for he wanted to marry. But this I could not do, though I offered to write and get his father's permission, and urge him again to return and look after his wife and family. So my letter was written and despatched, and we waited while it went on its long unknown journey to the mines where last we knew our friend had been labouring.

The months passed, and no answer came. At last there arrived in my post-bag my own letter to Mateyu. It had not been opened, but some native clerk who must have recognized my handwriting, and the postmark, had readdressed it and had written across the envelope " He is died."

This was black news, but it did not help me much. I required some official intimation of his death before I could dispose of the money I had in my keeping. So I told the son how the letter had returned, and that I was writing to the British Consul in this foreign land to get confirmation of his death.

Again we waited for many weeks, and at last came a letter to say that Mateyu had been imprisoned, and during the influenza epidemic he had disappeared. Another letter from a Nyasaland native to whom I had written said that Mateyu had been imprisoned along with others for killing a white man, and that he was supposed to be dead.

One day when I was meeting with my elders, I read to them all these letters, and asked them if they could find any trace of Mateyu, and confirmation of his death from any of their friends in this far away land. When I came out of the meeting, there was Mateyu at the door waiting for me—the same merry twinkle in his eyes, the same old impression of unlimited energy. The long years did not seem to have laid one line on his face, or turned one hair of his head.

He borrowed a shilling from me to take him home to his village, forty miles away, and promised to return and tell me his story. I gave him the money and waited impatiently for his coming that I might hear the news he had brought.

A week afterwards he appeared in my office, and this is the strange story he told. I do not vouch for the exact truth of it, for I have not heard the other side. An African has a marvellous power of telling his version of a fact, without diverging much from the truth, yet conveying an entirely wrong impression. But the tale is so romantic that I think it is worth telling as a story. Mateyu had tired of the store work to which he had first gone, and wandered farther afield to the lands where gold and copper were being discovered, and there he found more remunerative employment. His ' boss ' soon recognized that he was a boy with more intelligence and energy than most other workers, so he was made a foreman. Gradually he rose to be manager of a compound which was full of Nyasaland natives. Here he earned great wages, but found almost as great opportunities of spending them, and he saved almost nothing.

One Saturday afternoon he had cycled out to the European town that was in the neighbourhood, a town into which all the natives of the earth seem to have gathered. On his way back he was startled to see a dead body by the way-side, and when he had stopped and examined it, he recognized it to be the body of one of his Nyasaland boys. In haste he cycled back to his compound, and found it in a great state of excitement. The boys told him that a small party had gone to buy fish. On their way back they were attacked by local natives, who tried to take the fish from them. They did their best to keep their purchase, and one of them had been killed.

When he heard this story, Mateyu rode off to the nearest magistrate and reported the fracas. The magistrate said that he would come out the following day and make enquiries on the spot.

A Wanderer Returned

Next day the boys were produced and Mateyu, having given his story, called on those who had taken part in the fight to tell their story. When all were heard, the magistrate told the assembled natives that this was a very serious case, and they must go into the capital and give their evidence before the judge there. Mateyu was told to go at the head of those concerned, and to call at the "Witness house" where accommodation would be provided for them.

So the manager and his witnesses went forth in all confidence to the Court-House, and asked for the Witness Room. But their surprise was considerable when they found themselves lodged in prison and irons clapped on their feet and hands. Here they lived in no small bewilderment for some time. At length the trial was held, and after many witnesses had been heard, the judge turned fiercely to the Nyasaland witnesses and said :

"You natives of Nyasaland are for ever in trouble. You disturb the peace. The best thing I can do is to sentence each one of you to six years' imprisonment. Then perhaps your fellows will learn to keep quiet."

A Wanderer Returned

Mateyu, nothing daunted, asked why he and his friends should be imprisoned for having reported a crime. But he was sharply told that it would teach him to keep the peace if he spent a little while in prison. (This did not occur in a British colony, and one must remember that I have only heard Mateyu's story.) So the dazed crowd was led back to prison and chained. Some six weary months passed, and then influenza broke out among them. Seventy prisoners died, and the authorities becoming alarmed let all the others free, telling them to return to their compounds and report.

Mateyu went back to his, and was again appointed manager. No notice was taken of him by the police, and for a time it seemed as if the Government had forgotten the prisoners, until one day a Nyasaland boy who lived in town came to Mateyu and told him that the police were busy rounding up all the prisoners in the neighbourhood. Mateyu had no wish to spend five more years in prison, so he ran to his " boss," told him how things were, drew all the wages that were due to him, and mounting his bicycle he fled for Portuguese territory. Travelling day and night, through unknown bush country, he at last got safely across the border, and, feeling safe

A Wanderer Returned

from pursuit, tried to find work among the Portuguese settlers.

Again his industry and energy were appreciated, and he was given a place of trust. But his first wages were stolen from him, and his bicycle too disappeared. Then " he came to himself " and thought that home was best after all.

So he left Portuguese territory, and tried to cross to Nyasaland. But it was a long and perilous journey. He seems to have thought that the foreign Governments among whom he had sojourned were all in pursuit of him, and certainly he had no passes to save him from arrest at any point. He travelled by day, and, avoiding villages as far as he could, he slept in the trees at night, for he had no fire or light to guard him, and he was travelling alone.

At length after many adventures, he had crossed the border into Nyasaland, and now had arrived among his own people.

His home-coming was tragic enough. For when he arrived near where his once prosperous village stood, he found that it had been dispersed, and not a house was inhabitated. His wife was married to another man, for she had concluded he was dead.

A Wanderer Returned

His herd of cattle was all dead, not one beast remained. The money he had sent to his wife from time to time had been distributed among his relatives, and all was spent. Nothing remained to him but the money that was in my keeping ; cash, cattle, wife, children, even the village itself were scattered or had ceased to be.

Mateyu's reappearance made no small sensation. And without a day's delay he began to reconstruct his estate. His children gathered to him from the villages in which they lived ; his wife left her second husband and came to him. His relatives and connections assembled and talked of the new village that they must build. But there were things that could never be put together again. The relatives who had spent his money, and devoured his cattle, fled the country, afraid to face the man to whom they had been so false trustees. His wife returned and begged to be taken back. But he told her that she might live in his village, as a widow, no longer as his wife. His sons begged him with tears to take their mother back, but he only repeated his decision I spoke to him of the great love there once was between them, reminded him that she had more to forgive in him than he had in her, for he had not

been true to her during his long absence. I spoke
of the forgiveness of God only given as we forgive
others. But he hung his head and cried silently
as he said, " It cannot be."

Now he is busy with the reconstruction of his
village. And every day when he sits among the
villagers, or goes out to visit long separated friends
he says :

" Money is smoke. Wealth is like morning dew.
I had gold, fabulous wages, and now I have nothing.
All the best I had was lost when I sought for gold,
and gold was lost too. The Word of God is the
only thing that lasts, and is worth the seeking."

XI

WATERFINISHER—A CARRIER

"WATERFINISHER" is one of my favourite carriers. He is a fine specimen of an African, medium-sized, with calves like young fir trees, and a chest that stands out defiant, like the advertised production of some director of physical exercises. His face is covered with a short beard which is now tinged with grey. His skin is black as coal, and he has the voice of a megaphone which will not be silenced. Bubbling physical life, dancing, vociferous, joyful, makes his presence in our caravans like a gale of mountain wind.

In the early days when we used *machilas* (a hammock swung on a bamboo pole) he was one of the most tireless bearers. Sometimes when we were jogging along at the end of a twenty-five or thirty mile march, the men wearily shifting the pole from one shoulder to another, he would leap forward to relieve a distressed bearer, and, putting the bamboo on his shoulder, raise an ear-piercing yell which faded into a running song. Stretching his two arms straight up in the air, with his fingers quivering in rhythm, he would run and dance till he bounced the recumbent European up and down. Suddenly he would change his tactics, and turn right about facing the European, and dance a wild war dance. There was no remonstrating. You must simply hold on to the sides of the canvas and bear the wild tossing till his mad freak was over. Meanwhile he had convulsed the other bearers till they were shouting with laughter and song. Then he quickly changed position, and ran with the whole line behind him singing his chorus, and lightly trotting with a vigour that he had given them.

I was first fascinated with him because he bore a characteristic native name, which no new fangled western notions could make him alter. For, indeed, the roll-call of a native caravan is a most incongruous mixture. When you start out on a journey in our land it is not a matter of calling a taxi, into which you bundle your portmanteaux, and then drive away, watching an ugly dial measure out your twopences, while a man, curiously indifferent to

all human interest in you, twists and turns your
car amid the traffic.

In Africa you must prepare your tent and bedding
and food boxes, and your pots and pans, and call up
a score of carriers. Early in the morning there is
bustle outside your house, for all the carriers you
have engaged are there, and dozens of others who
hope that an extra man or two may be required.
You give to each his bundle, and write on your
paper the name of the carrier and of his load.
Mkuzo and Pemba and Vumazonke are there,
Moses and Yesaya and Jeremiah, Matches and Jam
and Sago, a mixture of music and prose, of prophets
and patriarchs, and of all the groceries of the stores.
Any one with an ear for music and a sense of fitness
will rejoice when a real African name is given, and
what could be more like the genuine article than
Majimara, the " Waterfinisher " ?

At the end of a long day's march we might camp
by the edge of some wood. As the men arrive they
throw down their loads, and sit beside them on the
ground. Waterfinisher is one of the first in. He
has just squatted, and wiped the perspiration from
his body, when he draws from a little squirrel skin,
which hangs about his girdle, a little snuff gourd,

and taps out the snuff into the palm of his left hand. With the first finger and the thumb of his right hand he fills his wide nostrils with snuff. A wild cough ending in a song proclaims his exhilaration, and the tears roll down his cheeks. The snuff boxes go round, and soon a look of peaceful rest comes over the tired carriers.

Some go forth to gather dry wood, and throw huge logs into a heap. A fire is kindled, and by and by bursts from blinding smoke into cheerful blaze. Earthenware pots filled with water are placed on the fire and slowly boil. The maize meal is sprinkled into the boiling water and vigorously stirred. Waterfinisher always seems to gather the work about his own person. He takes a pot out of the fire, and holding it with the soles of his feet, with a leaf between them and the hot pot to prevent his skin from singeing, he stirs and stirs till the mass of porridge is ready. Then it is dished out in leaves, and the carriers gather in groups about the food and eat it with their fingers. A gourd of water is now passed round, and each man has a huge drink, which is followed by certain vulgar sounds proclaiming their fulness and satisfaction with the meal.

Waterfinisher—A Carrier

The snuff goes round again and again while the men sit about the fire. Up to this point there has been comparative silence. During the meal jaws were working hard, but there was no sound of human speech. Now the talk begins and grows till the camp fires ring with story and laughter. Above all the noise Waterfinisher may be heard booming out his conversation. He seems to be talking to a crowd five hundred yards away. When the night grows later I call for silence that I may sleep, and the noise drops away, but soon Waterfinisher has something he must say and you can hear his whispered yell resounding in the woods, and ending in a roar of laughter, which shows that all injunctions to silence have been forgotten.

As the years moved on Waterfinisher increased in knowledge, for he attended school along with his little children. After laborious pursuit of elusive letters he was able to read the Gospel, and as he had made confession of his faith in Christ, he was received into the Church. Then his lung power made itself felt in public service, for when we sang our African music you could sometimes hear one voice, incapable of modulation, roaring over the mass of sound, and in the heart of the congregation,

Waterfinisher—A Carrier

Waterfinisher with twinkling eyes, chest out, swaying body, could be seen making the most joyful noise.

I had him taught to be a top sawyer, for he had intelligence and strength enough for this heavy job. The saw-pit was a merry place when he was there. Standing on his log, with a dance he drew up the long blade, and then let it swing down to the pull of the underman. There was a rhythm of movement of man and saw that made the whole process a poem set to the music of ripping wood.

He has a wonderful family. Eight, nine, ten have appeared, handsome little brown boys and girls. The elder are growing into manhood now, but still they come. Almost every year he kneels at the baptismal font with a dainty morsel of chocolate-coloured humanity, wrapped in a yard of grey calico, and looking so fragile in his brawny arms. But there have been sad days in that family too. First his brightest and best, a cook in a European household, died. And then his second, a teacher, lost his wife a few weeks after his marriage. Then the strong man was silent. I stood beside him at the graves. No cry came from his lips, though that is the safety valve for the emotion of the African in the day of his bitter sorrow. But the tears were on his face, and he sang the hymn by the grave with a softness that seemed tragically different from his usual boisterousness. Once or twice I tried to speak some words of comfort to him when we travelled together, and he listened silently, making no reply but that a shy, quiet smile stole over his rugged face.

Time, however, has great healing powers. Once more his voice booms out like the wild ocean wave breaking on the rocks. There is not always work for him at the saw-pit, so in his idle months he still travels with me on my frequent journeys. His favourite load now is the tent, for it is soft and yielding on the shoulders or the head. He lifts it as a very little thing, and carries it off with a run and a shout. You may be sure that when you arrive at the camping ground, whoever may be late or footsore, Waterfinisher will be in time, the earliest and the freshest to arrive.

One clings to him because he has shown that his heart is as tender as a child's. One day I had a severe touch of malaria while I was walking behind my carriers, and finally had to lie down beside a bush, where I became very ill. Waterfinisher was disturbed when I did not arrive with the others, and turned back on his tracks to seek me. When he found me under the bush he carried me gently to the tent and put me to bed. Through that night, while the fever was at its height, he and another sat on the floor on either side of my bed antici- pating every want. Should I move, or even raise my hand, they were on their knees at once to give me anything I might want. While the fever lasted no nurse could have tended me more faithfully.

But when all goes well what a roaring torrent of talk can rush from his capacious mouth ! I some- times wish he would fall asleep a little faster, and let me do likewise. What does he talk about ? I have heard a European say that the African talks of nothing but cattle and women. That was because he could only recognize these two words in the clamour of their " friendly yells." But, believe me, it is not true. For the Christian lad especially speaks with a delicacy that could offend no sensitive ear. One night the carriers were hospitably given a hut close by my tent to sleep in. When bed time came there was an uproar of discussion. It was no simple story relieved by mimicry that held them, but a keen debate, which was cooled when it grew hottest by a roar of laughter. I was tired and

longed for sleep, so I shouted to them to be quiet.
Immediately dead silence fell upon the village.
Soon, however, whispered conversation could be
heard, and Waterfinisher began his subdued shout,
which ended in full lung power, all the stops out.
I called again, and quiet reigned for a few moments,
until the debate began again, and Waterfinisher
was audible above them all. Thought ran furiously
and refused to be dammed. At last I rose, and
going to the hut remonstrated with effect.

Next morning when we tramped through the
wood, I said to Waterfinisher, who walked in front
of me, "What exciting debate did you hold last
night?"

"Debate?" he roared, "It was over a pair of
trousers."

"What troubled you about them?" I asked.

"The owner of the house had left a pair hanging
upon a line," he shouted back to me. "Some said
he did that out of pure swank to show his wealth,
and some said he did it because there was no better
place to put them. We argued about his motive.
What do you say made him do it?"

"Well, I fancy you were his guests," I replied,
"and you should have remembered that, and not

discussed the man who lent you his hut so hospitably. I expect he heard you, for your talk was fairly audible."

Waterfinisher gave a shout of laughter and said, " Yes, we were rude."

I walked along the road wondering how many psychologists could get more excited over an analysis of motive than our naked carriers had been.

XII

THE BELOVED MADMAN

ONCE or twice messages came to me from an old "induna" called Bellows, urging us to open a school in his head village, and finally a deputation of young men arrived to press the invitation on us. Not many years before, the Mission had only been tolerated in the country. Then the toleration changed to a reluctant permission to teach. But a short time of active work was enough to convince the people that a most precious treasure was in the mission's hands, and soon invitations to occupy were pouring in. Few moments are more thrilling for the missionary than those when a hermit district throws open its doors and calls for occupation. And such a call had come from villages under Bellows' sway. So one day I marched off to his village to make arrangements for the settling of teachers there.

Old Bellows was a delightful African gentleman. The years had multiplied upon him till his body was bent, and he moved about leaning on a staff. Merry smiles constantly lit up his seamed and wrinkled face, like sunlight on furrowed waters. His courtesy to strangers was perfect, though I fancy that over his suavity the people had often seen a tornado of passion rage.

As my acquaintance with him deepened, his evident pleasure in my visits often made me find excuses for turning aside, and spending a night in his village. Then the formal dignified greeting of the NGONI was forgotten, and he would seize my hand, and kiss it, as he poured out a voluble welcome.

He had many a story of the long wanderings of his people, for he had crossed the Zambesi with the army far back in last century. He was then a lad herding cattle, and now he was an old man between eighty and ninety years of age. What a history of fighting and burning, of long marches, and long idleness, of repletion and starvation filled in these years!

He died only a few years ago with the evangelist praying by his bedside. The message of the Gospel had come to him in his old age, when the ingrained habits of many years had become part of his life.

The Beloved Madman

And although he did not break with some of these, such as polygamy, and so was never received into the Church, I like to think that perhaps he was in the Kingdom of God. For happily the Kingdom is wider than the Church, and the names of some who have never been baptized may be written in the Lamb's Book of Life.

One saw in him a gentle courtesy, a patient forbearance, a sunshine heart, pleasure in a talk about God, and a readiness to pray, that seemed to show how, through the thicket and tangle of long ignorance, God had found a way to his soul.

On the day of my expedition to open his school, we had only seen one another once or twice. At first we had approached with much ceremony, saluting him with the cry " Komo," which is given to great *indunas* of the paramount chief. But in a few minutes he had fairly captured me, and I judged him to be the kindliest old gentleman I had met in Africa, so we now entered the village with assurance and confidence.

As soon as we reached the outskirts of his village, the bustle and sounds of a red-letter day were evident and audible. The large village was swarming with people. Many children were of course in the foreground, the first to see us and to meet us, other young lads shouting their greeting. That was the inverse order of formality. The children should have been hidden away, the lads should wait for their elders. Among the huts groups of women were gathered, struggling between a curiosity to see the white man and a timidity that drove them suddenly to hide behind the houses.

Instead of sitting down at the kraal gate, as the custom is, to wait for our reception, we passed rapidly into the village, and dismounted at the door of the *induna's* hut. Bellows was sitting under the eaves with one or two of his old wives, and while he welcomed me, the crowds in the village rapidly assembled in a wide circle round us, none venturing too near, out of respect for their headman. A few of the senior and more important villagers came up to me one by one, and, kneeling on the ground, greeted me, and then withdrew.

At length the time came to open the business, and talk about the school which we hoped to begin. So I stood forth and explained how the villagers must help themselves if we gave them a school. They must build a good house and keep it in repair. They must pay school fees and feed the teachers who might be sent to them from a distance. For we were not there to pauperize them but to stimulate the spirit of self-help. And experience has taught us plainly enough that the results of their own labour are far more precious than the generous and costly gifts of Europe.

I spoke of what the school stood for, and how we should expect to see results in the overthrow of evil customs, such as drunkenness, licentious dances, polygamy, and in the observing of gentle laws and sweet manners, and in the following of Jesus Christ.

I now think it is a mistake to make the negatives so plain. For the legal minded African seizes on these as the sum of Christianity, and forgets to lay the greatest emphasis on the positive virtues. But full healthy life is the best negation of disease, and the man who finds the beauty of Christ is the best hater of sin.

Old Bellows, and one or two of his counsellors followed, commending what I had said, and promising to do their best to make the school a success.

It takes time to initiate a new movement. Sudden action after brief explanation is the foreign way.

The Beloved Madman

In Africa we talk all round the subject first. The more we ventilate it, the freer will be its movement. Nothing is more fatal to natural growth than sudden planting, which has not been preceded by turning the soil well in long palaver, and sunning it by abundant discussion.

When the seniors had finished their harangues a young blacksmith rose. I recognized him as the most earnest and urgent man in the deputation that had recently been pressing me to open a school. What he wanted to say was that the school, and the Gospel, were meant for the old people as well as for the young, and that the grown men and women should hear the call to give up practices that were contrary to the Word of God. An earnest and sensible word worth uttering.

But he had not yet finished, when we were all startled by a wild figure, who dashed into the open space, like a mad bull, and in confused tangled fashion began to yell and denounce the blacksmith for his impertinence. All order was swept away by this hurricane of excitement. Everywhere the people buzzed with talk, others ran here and there, while the enraged savage danced and shouted incoherent nonsense. Then he rushed through the crowd and dived into a neighbouring hut. "Who is this?" I asked someone beside me. "It is the *induna's* eldest son, Little Meal. He has mad fits."

I had scarcely got this explanation when Little Meal reappeared, this time stark naked, carrying his shield and spear. He danced wildly, denouncing all the time the blacksmith who had dared to say that the old people must give up their established practices. Then he threw himself upon an ash heap, digging his face into it, snorting like a wild bull, and whitening his body with the ash.

Throughout this exhibition old father Bellows sat quite undisturbed, muttering a little about the folly of his son, but the crowd was terrified, and many fled. Then one of the wives of Little Meal came forward, gave him a blow and a shove, and a good deal of abuse, and sent him very humbly back to his hut to dress himself and lay aside his weapons.

This was my first introduction to Little Meal. In the years that followed we became great friends, and he proved himself a most energetic, though erratic, helper of the school.

For Little Meal is not always mad, though he is always eccentric. His danger periods come when he has been drinking and gets excited. Then he may dash into the kraal and stab the cattle with his spear. One day he became so bold that he bit his wife's thumb deeply. But the woman told the magistrate of her grievance and had the triumph of seeing her husband sentenced to some months' imprisonment. That was a very disturbing day to Little Meal when he heard the sentence. However, he soon adjusted himself to his new circumstances, and only visited the prison at night to sleep there, while outside in the village street he met his friends and received their gifts of food. Sometimes he strolled along to the magistrate's bungalow to have a gossip with him.

Through all these months he was compelled to abstain from beer, and he grew in bodily and mental health. And so great is his confidence in the European that he will take punishment or reward with equal gratitude, believing that it is the best way for him, seeing that the European has so judged. Every year now he visits the Government station to pay his respects to the magistrate who imprisoned him, and to give him some little present.

Twice he has been for long periods in our hospital. The first time he made a good recovery from a painful and enervating disease that had

154

disturbed his mental balance not a little. The second time it was for cataract he came, and the doctor successfully operated on one eye. He lay or sat about for several days bandaged up, very patient, but for a longing for beer which he was warned he must not touch. At last the day came when the bandages were removed and the eye looked well and healthy. Next day, however, the doctor was surprised to find it red and inflamed. She was puzzled and annoyed with the set back, but soon the native dispenser revealed the whole story.

Little Meal, rejoicing in his recovery, and the removal of the bandages, sent his wife out to the neighbouring villages to procure a pot of beer. She was successful in her hunt, and she and he spent the long night celebrating the return of sight with a grand carousal.

" Didn't the doctor tell you that you might lose your sight if you drank ? " said the dispenser.

But Little Meal was not disturbed. " I cannot lose my sight," he answered, " for the doctor cut out the disease, and she showed my wife the little white ball she had taken out of my eye. If the disease is no longer there, how can I lose my sight ? "

The Beloved Madman

Old father Bellows is dead now, and with him has passed the last of that generation that crossed the Zambesi in 1837, and Little Meal reigns in his stead. So strong and intimate is the African loyalty to blood, he suffers little loss of power or prestige by his eccentricities or madness.

Happily his bubbling, restless energy has found a vent in public work. Was it not he who drove his people forth with clubs in his hand, and wild threats on his tongue, to hoe roads between his villages? Where is there a larger or more decorated school in all the tribe than the one in his head village? Day by day he gathered his people and compelled them to work, until he had completed a very handsome building, and decorated it within and without with red and white clay.

One day I was an unwilling witness of his irrepressible energy. We were holding a series of meetings in his church and he had stalked in through the crowded audience. He was a most comical figure, gaunt and bent, with spectacles on his squat nose, and an old blue cloth girt loosely about his body, and he wore a look of preternatural solemnity. Making his way up to the platform he sat behind me all through the service with immobile grave

The Beloved Madman

face, until the last hymn was given out. At that moment all his power of restraint came to an end, and, rising to his feet, he proceeded to address the congregation. Beginning quietly enough, he spoke of the need of public roads. Then he gradually got excited, and after referring to the lack of ready obedience, he cried : " In the old days if a slave would not obey his chief he would be killed."

So he ended with a shout, and stalked through the congregation, repeating in vociferous tones, " He would be killed. He would be killed."

I saw him pass along outside the building, spectacles on the knob of his flat nose, the solemn, eager look still on his face, as he made his way to the village, having delivered his soul. And the refrain still tumbled from his lips, " He would be killed. He would be killed."

When I camp outside his village he abstains from beer, for he knows that drinking excites him. If I come unexpectedly, and he has been drinking that day, he hides himself until morning. Then he visits my tent two or three times a day and talks with great repetition of the things that obsess his mind at the moment. At each visit he brings a present, such as a fowl, or a dish of maize porridge, as an excuse for his coming. This gives him the privilege of begging without shame.

Happily his wants are simple, and a spoonful of salt or sugar, or a sheet of paper send him away well content. He cannot read or write, but he has great faith in the magical authority of the written word. So he must have paper, that when he sends a message to anyone, it may not be by word of mouth, but by the written word, which he gets a teacher or educated friend to put on paper.

I try to be as hospitable to him when he comes to my station, though I beg nothing in return. Yet no gift is wasted on Little Meal. Every fowl, or sheep or basket of fruit that he has received from me he has treasured in a faultless memory. For years afterwards he will tell his people and remind me of what I gave him on each visit.

XIII

FROM DEATH TO LIFE

GREAT WIND was dying. But that was not the name given him by his father. Several times during his stormy life he had changed his name, calling himself something new when he would commemorate a great incident in his career. By his last name he would have people remember how wild and stormy a chief he was, breaking the feeble and bending the strong. For by the power of his spear he had gathered his villages, and with his flashing eye and fierce growl he had made his cruellest verdicts final, against which there could be no appeal. Now he was stricken and dying like his meanest slave.

The hut was crowded with his weeping wives, in the arms of one of whom he sat back gasping out his life. His headman was there too, asking him during moments of consciousness what was to be done with his property, whom he named as his successor, and, last and most terrible, who had bewitched him to bring him to this terrible pass.

Outside the people sat in silent groups, which were constantly increased by new arrivals from distant villages. For the news had spread that Great Wind was seriously ill, and loyalty or fear had drawn about him sad and terrified representatives from all the relatives and from dependent villages.

The doctors had visited him, and when their medicines had failed, had fallen back on the last resort of the ignorant, declaring that magic had been at work, and the chief was bewitched.

Neither Faith nor Science had yet come to comfort or relieve. Thus, in a wild, dark night of superstition, Great Wind was passing from the land where he ruled through the gates that none could close.

At length the end came. His wives closed his eyes and stretched out his body, moaning all the time. Their cry reached to those outside, and in a few minutes the village was pandemonium. Silent Death had summoned the Furies, and they made their voices heard. Men were now on their feet, with hands clasped above their heads, covering

A CHARACTERISTIC VILLAGE IN ITS RAMSHACKLE UNTIDINESS

To the left are the poles of the open cattle kraal, the heart of the village. The grass over the doorway of the hut to the right has been pulled out by lazy people to make fire-lighters or to serve as candles. Mortars for pounding maize lie about,

From Death to Life

themselves with shields, and crying, with soul-rending wail: "*Tata wae! Tata wae!*" ("Alas, my father! alas, my father!") The women took up the chorus, prolonging the "Alas!" through cries that rose and fell in a wailing chant.

Here and there men and women were fighting, striking at some poor slave whose magical powers were suspected, and already some accused folk were in flight through the bush, running for their lives to some distant tribe where they might be safe.

For magic is a safeguard of chieftainship. Where secret enemies are everywhere, lusting for the blood of the chief who has oppressed them, it is well for him that a misty belief walls him round about. Magic stands guard about his life, and many a time has turned the assassin aside. Yet she cannot forbid the coming of death, and now Great Wind has passed:

> "His life a general mist of error,
> His death a hideous storm of terror."

Next day the funeral takes place. To all the great men interested messengers have reported the death and then fled, lest the anger of sorrow and suspicion should lay avenging hands on them.

From Death to Life

The witch-doctor, too, has been busy, and secretly he has whispered to the headman the names of wives and slaves who shall be buried with Great Wind. For in the dark land to which he has gone he must not live as a slave. Wives shall go with him to give him consolation, and slaves to serve him, that he may not wander alone.

So men have crept about in the dark, and have seized half a dozen women and tied them together, and closed them into a hut to wait there till the funeral. They know well what fate awaits them, but they are led out in the funeral procession with stolid, stupid looks, dazed in the presence of their coming death.

Vibisi is one of them, a comely young woman, who has yet had no husband of her own. She is but a slave, captured in war, and the property of the dead man. She moaned through the night her wail for the chief, but the tears that flowed down her face were not pity for her late sovereign lord, but piercing sorrow for the sudden close that was to come to all her life and hopes.

A hole has been broken in the hut where the body lay, and through this aperture the chief is borne, and all his little possessions, his stool, his shield and

162

spear, the clothes he has worn, and his musical instruments. When the procession starts, a wail rises from the hundreds who have gathered, " *Tata wae !* *Tata wae !* " and for a mile away it can be heard, the note of hopeless loss rising and falling like the moaning of the sea.

The procession moves on at a trot till they come to the grave which has been dug in a thick tangle of bush. Then the killing begins, under the direction of the presiding witch-doctor. One and another of the women have already been laid at the bottom of the grave to make a couch for the dead master. Then Vibisi is led forth, stupid with terror. As she is brought to the edge of the grave the dust of the dry earth enters her nostrils, and she sneezes violently. At this the witch-doctor steps forth and stops the executioner, who stands ready with his knob-kerry. The spirits have spoken in that sneeze. Vibisi must not be killed ; they will not leave her in the company of the chief.

So her bonds are unloosed, and she wanders back to the village, dazed, and scarcely aware of the strange deliverance she has had from death. For the air is full of the death wail. And all through

From Death to Life

that day and night it still goes on: "*Tata wae!
Tata wae!*"

For days after when the sun rises the women
weep aloud, and again when the sun goes down.
The wives of the dead live by themselves; they
have bound filthy cloths about their heads, and
neither wash nor pay any attention to their bodies.
The village is unswept, and every day is growing
more loathsomely dirty. Beer in little gourds
has been carried to the grave, and poured down
a hollow reed which rises from the mouth of
the dead up to the top of the grave mound, that
the spirit may have his accustomed drink. Scraps
of cloth have been laid there for his clothing in
the other world, and one or two dishes of maize
porridge.

The field mice have now found out this provision,
and begin to nibble it. So in the morning, when
the villagers come to the grave they see that some
of the food has been consumed, and they turn back
to tell their friends that the spirit of the dead is
friendly, for he has eaten what was given him.
Now they can live quietly, believing that the dead
chief comes to them in their need, and sees that all
goes well with them.

From Death to Life

In the broken hut they place another pot of beer, and watch, for it will be well for them if he will live within the village and defend them from all the lurking enemies of the dark underworld who may harm them.

One day a little boy calls out that a snake has entered the hut. It wriggled out from the cattle kraal fence and slithered across the courtyard, among the dirt of maize cobs and leaves and rubbish, and disappeared within the dismantled house of the dead. Then smiles replace all fears, for was not this the spirit returning to his former dwelling-place? One woman enters quietly and looks at the fermented beer which has foamed down the sides of the gourd and dried there. The cockroaches have been busy, and scurry away at her approach. And she comes forth to confirm them that all is well. A good and friendly spirit has come to dwell within their village, and has drunk their beer.

Now the great witch-doctor is summoned. He orders the village to be swept clean. Heaps of rubbish and broken pots are carried out to the cross-ways. The hearths of the huts are swept, and the smouldering logs are carried out to the rubbish heap. All fire is extinguished. Medicines have been pre-

From Death to Life

pared and are sprinkled on all the huts, to protect them from magical evil. Then with great ceremony the witch-doctor makes a new fire by friction. A dry log catches, and from this other sticks are kindled, and soon the hearths of all the huts are cheerful with crackling fires.

The mourning is over. The dark cloud that sat upon the village has lifted. Barbers are busy shaving the heads and faces of the mourners. The filthy rags are burned, and all go to the river to wash.

That night there is a scene of boisterous revelry in the village, for great gourds of beer have been set to which all are welcome. Dances have begun in the open courtyard, which grow more furious and more loathsome as the night advances. At length the morning breaks on a village in which drunken people are sleeping off the debauchery of the past night before resuming their carousals in the evening.

So death has come and gone. It left no sanctifying comfort, and little hope. It has only added one more terror to the darkness, and given one more excuse for nights of brutish revelry.

But where is Vibisi in all the revelry ? You may

166

From Death to Life

seek her among the crowds of dancing, drunken women, but you will not find her. She is now a person apart, consecrated to the tribal god who lives in the mist-capped mountain. Far away from all the villages, in a hut by herself, she lives her solitary life, waiting for the god to visit her.

The joy of mourning ended has worked itself out, and the village settles down to normal life again. But quiet has not followed. For sometimes, when belated villagers were passing through the wood a crackling of branches has been heard, and the frightened traveller took a little twig and broke it, and cast it into the bush, to answer the spirits that were playing tricks with him in the dark.

Blind worms have once or twice crossed the paths of the people who had started out on a journey, and they have returned and laid their burdens down, afraid to go farther after so evil an omen.

There has been sickness, too, and children have been dying. Yet there were those sure signs that the dead chief was friendly. Some more potent spirit must be working against them.

At last the great priest of the tribe is summoned. He is a village headman, but his father before him,

From Death to Life

and his grandfather too, always acted as priest of the tribe when they would address the great hill-god, and he must go with them. No other may speak. He only is the advocate of the people.

So in a solemn procession he leads them to the hut of the hill-god's wife to talk with her and offer sacrifice. Vibisi sees the long procession winding up the bush path to her lonely hut, and withdraws from sight.

Presently they arrive and sit before her.

"O wife of the hill-god," the priest calls, "we have come to talk with the great spirit, and give him whatever he may require of us."

From within the hut a small, frightened voice asks: "And who are ye who would speak with The Howling One?"

"We are the children of Great Wind."

A shiver of alarm shakes the poor lone woman as she thinks of the day when she was taken from among the dead.

"Has the hill-god come to you?" asks the priest.

"Yes, once he came," replies the woman.

"And how did he come?"

"He came with the sound of a rushing wind,

breaking his way through the maize fields. You may see his track in the broken stalks."

" What like was he when he came ? " asked the priest.

" Like a great snake with a fierce red head."

" What did you do when you saw him come ? "

" I swept my hut and put forth all fire, then I sat in the dark, my head covered, and trembled at his approach."

" Ah ! " said the high priest of the tribe, " she has indeed seen the god, and he has visited the wife we gave him."

Then he brought the offerings of beer, and coloured beads, and a young ox, and, leaving these for the god, he prayed in the name of the tribe, asking that he would be friendly to them, and turn aside all malignant forces that harassed them.

The years passed bringing great changes with them. A wild race of warriors swept down upon them and overwhelmed the feeble people over whom Great Wind had ruled. When they heard of the approach of the marauding horde they prayed to the hill-god, and offered sacrifice, but he had not heard, for he was feeble in comparison with the Great Spirit who guided the raiding armies.

From Death to Life

So the tribe left him to neglect, disappointed
with his abilities to help, and now they prayed
with the conquerors to the ancestral spirit of their
nation.

Gods with us have their day. Even they are not
immortal. The spirits of the great dead who
haunted the wood and the village are soon forgotten. By the third generation they have passed
out of the memory of men. And the gods of the
pools or hills who have not been equal to an
emergency are dismissed from the worship of the
tribe.

So Vibisi returned to her own people; all the
reverence and awe which secluded her had passed,
and she became as one of themselves, and became
the wife of a man in the village.

She was an old widow when the missionary came
to preach among her people, and she sat in wondering awe of the strangely dressed white man. His
tongue was certainly foreign, almost as foreign as
his dress. Words came from his lips, but she, an
old woman, could never learn his new language.
So that day passed, and it had never occurred to
her that perhaps the language he spoke was her
own.

From Death to Life

In the evening a native teacher spoke with her. He was like herself, with a dark face, a man who ate maize porridge and lived in a round hut like hers. She knew his mother and his father. Yes, he was one of her own people, so when he spoke her mind lay open to hear him. Had she heard the white Teacher speak? Yes, she had seen him and heard him.

"What did he tell you?"

"Am I a European that I should understand the white man's language?"

"But he spoke your own tongue."

"Did he? Ah! there is no end of the wisdom of these white men. They are not people like us. God has been very kind to them."

"Well, you must keep your ears open to-morrow, and listen to what he says, for he is God's own messenger."

Next morning Vibisi was there among the women, sitting on the ground when the missionary held his village service. After he had been speaking for some time, the sound of his words struck her as familiar, though the form was stiff and foreign. She strained to hear. What was this he spoke of? "Life everlasting." Then we do not die when sickness takes us ? " Is there something beyond the dark gate through which Great Wind passed and from which I was drawn back just as I was about to pass in ? "

The question worried her. That night she dreamed of a land that is fairer than day, and she saw One who came and took her hand, and asked her to follow.

When the morning broke she sought out the native teacher and told him of her dream, and asked where she too must go to find the life that never ends. Day by day the teacher taught her, and little by little the light began to break on her dark soul. Until at length she was rejoicing in the great possession. The God of Heaven and Earth had come to visit her, and she had swept her house and offered it to Him. Now indeed was she the wife of a God, and she called Him her Husband and Lord.

> " Tears shall take comfort and turn gems,
> And wrongs repent to diadems."

See her to-day. It is a great day of the sacrament of the Lord's Supper. Within the big church a thousand men and women are waiting devoutly for the serving of the Body and Blood. As the elders

From Death to Life

pass in their white dresses, handing bread and wine to the simple Christians there, the heads go down and hands cover the eyes of those who have partaken. Among them sits Vibisi, an old white-haired grannie who had tasted the bitterness of death, and now is receiving the Bread of Life, of which if one eat he shall never die. And as she bows her head and covers her eyes her heart beats in humble anticipation, for her Lord God has come to visit her, and she is still to hear what He may say.

XIV

MAN'S GRATITUDE TO MAN

THERE is no good so sweet as that which comes after long effort and pain. The bleakest land stretches out arms of welcome to the storm-driven sailor. The hardest bed is a kingly couch to the traveller physically tired. Correctly balanced books are a poem after long hunts for elusive pennies.

One day when we straggled down to the Valley, after seven hours' toilsome tumbling over stony hills and through thorn thickets, with a blazing sun overhead, and no water to drink for thirty miles, there met us on the path three women bearing great calabashes of water. They knew we should arrive that day, and they had walked out three or four miles to meet us, carrying this precious gift. When did water taste more like nectar, or Christianity, which had created so great thoughtfulness in these poor women, seem more lovely?

In contrast to the hot valley, our plateau some-

Man's Gratitude to Man

times appears to us like a land of Canaan, flowing with milk and honey, on which the sun smiles gently, and through which life-giving breezes blow, where men walk not afraid, a land greatly to be desired. But I write this in the Highlands of Scotland, where, too, there are sun, moon, and stars, and a wind on the heath, and a free people with soft speech and gentle manners, and perhaps this, too, is a land greatly to be desired. Yet when we climb out of the scorching Loangwa Valley, where water is hard to find, and dangerous to drink, where the tsetse fly pierces like a red-hot needle, and trees close us in on all sides, and the poor people, hunted for generations, are feeble and cringing, Ngoniland is a paradise by contrast.

But paradise is not reached without pain and struggle. So we thought one day after we had been climbing and descending barren quartz-covered hills on our way back to the plateau. Grass fires had burnt the vegetation. The ground was blackened, and even the sharp white quartz was browned by the fierce heat that had raged over it. The trees were leafless and scorched. The sun blazed overhead, and the stony path burned the feet of the weary travellers.

Man's Gratitude to Man

The river where we might camp and cook was still far ahead. The sun went down, and darkness began to close us round. Still on we trudged, expecting that each new dip would reveal the long desired stream, only to find at the bottom of the valley boulders and stones that gave no help to our thirst. My wife, a young bride, recently out from the comforts of civilization, with its trains and tea-rooms, followed behind me at the head of our caravan. Spent and tired beyond speech, she struggled on, with visions of dainty drawing-room teas, and hot baths, and refreshing changes. But the reality was there, a narrow stone-strewn track, a dry steep land, and darkness creeping over all.

The night had grown so dark that when I put on my jacket to protect myself from the chill, she begged me to take it off again, so that my white shirt at least might give her some indication of our route.

At last we did arrive, but not to daintiness and rest. The stream was but a marsh, and the hills ran down to it through long dripping grass. Our tent was hastily pitched in the darkness, on a lumpy slope among the wet grass, and a poor fire was kindled, over which a scrappy meal was cooked.

Man's Gratitude to Man

Then we turned in to find our rest and refreshment in the oblivion of sleep.

Next morning at earliest dawn, while the air was still chilly and our bodies stiff and half frozen, we started off again. Soon the sun rose over the trees, the mists melted away and we found ourselves in a pleasant glade which ran gently, without interruption, down to the Rukuru River, and then to the paradise we had seen before us.

We now lay in our *machilas*, and our bearers carried us at a swift trot, with rhythmical song, new spirit and energy sending them on with light springing steps. Soon we were across the river and among the populous villages. Our tent was pitched, our goods laid out in orderly array, the table laid with a tempting breakfast. The misery of the past days was all forgotten now in the pleasure of our arrival, while the hospitable people spread before us presents of foodstuffs for ourselves and our men, and best of all a tin of foaming fresh milk.

Here we rested for a day, rejoicing in the land and its people. Next day there began a series of services, preparatory to the celebration of the sacraments. Hundreds of folk had gathered from the outlying villages, crowding out the large school in which I preached three times a day. Then came the great Sabbath with its multitudes, and sacraments, and services of big import.

By seven o'clock the paths were alive with long files of white-robed folk, converging from all sides on the open space where the school stood. When the main service should begin the whole neighbourhood was humming with humanity. No building could hold the vast congregation, so we met outside. A white cloth was spread over a table, and there the baptismal font was set. In front of it a few score of adults were arranged, who this day were to be received into the Church by baptism. Behind them, and all around them, the congregation seated themselves. Up two great ant-hills they swarmed as into a gallery. On the top, the chief and headman had found places from which they could view the crowds and watch the strange ceremony that was to take place.

That was a great day. The people had travelled many miles to be present, and would not be content with a snippety sermon. They must have value for their trouble. So the service went on, the sermon was preached, the catechumens were addressed and received in baptism, yet there was no

Man's Gratitude to Man

movement, no sign of impatience under the hot sun, from which they had no shelter.

At last the time came when we must close. Yet it was hard to stop. What infinite appeal there was in the thousands gathered there! Old men and women who had passed through bloodshed, through slavery and drudgery, to whom no light and peace from God had yet come. Headmen in whose hands lay the destiny of their villages. Young lads and girls, with all the days before them, promising degrading indulgence, or uplifting, expanding life from God. Their inarticulate cry pierced one. Again I mounted a chair to make another passionate appeal for doors to be opened that the King of Glory might come in. At length voice and body could hold out no longer, and the Benediction was pronounced over the awe-struck multitude.

In the evening we gathered about the white covered table, on which there stood this time the vessels of communion. And there in the evening peace, those who had acknowledged Christ as Lord and Saviour, took His Body and Blood, and we spoke together of the gifts and graces of the King of Love.

Man's Gratitude to Man

On Monday morning my wife found that the headman of our caravan was ill with pneumonia, the result of the strain and exposure of the past days. She could not nurse him properly in the discomfort of a crowded village hut. So she put him into my *machila* and started out for the deserted station at Hora, twenty miles away, where he and she could be more comfortable. As neither of us was feeling very bright, we parted with some misgiving,—I to tramp some sixty miles back to my station, and she to wait on her patient.

All went well for some hours while I pushed on at the head of my load men, enjoying the ever-changing scenes of the bush path. But after we had covered a few miles I began to feel sick and faint. So I slackened my pace, and one by one the carriers passed me until I was now in the rear of the column. Malarial fever had evidently gripped me after the exposure of the valley, and it was rapidly developing. My pace slowed down until I could only stagger along, and my caravan passed out of sight and hearing.

Violent spasms of sickness came on, and I lost all trace of the path. Lying down sometimes in the shade of a tree until the spasm passed, utterly unaware of the direction of the path, I tumbled about in the thick bush trying to find my way back. We were in the middle of a wide belt of scrub which had grown over deserted gardens, and I knew of no villages within several miles. I had a constant sense that safety lay in getting back to the path, and now I was so ill that I could only crawl on my hands and knees. This I continued to do in a vain effort to find the little winding footpath where men walked. At last I could go no farther, and lay under a shady bush and lost consciousness.

The sun was going down in the west when I was awakened by voices. I looked up to find four or five of the carriers bending over me. They had marched on without a halt to the first village, never doubting that I was following close behind, and then they sat down to wait for me. When the hours passed and I had not appeared they began to be anxious, and some of them had retraced their steps, looking carefully for the spoor of my boots among the native footsteps. With the keen eyes of practised hunters, they picked out my spoor, saw where I had turned aside and followed the marks of my blundering wanderings, and had found me asleep under the shrub.

Man's Gratitude to Man

They carried me on to the village where my tent had been erected, and my bed made, and tucked me in. All that night two of them took turns of sitting beside me. So careful and tender was their watch that I could not move a hand, scarcely open an eyelid, without my nurse rising and watching anxiously for any need I might have.

Under such circumstances you prove how deep is the reverent care that your men may have for you, and how precious a possession the European master is to his native followers. Men speak scornfully of the lack of gratitude in the African. I know a little about these simple children of nature, and can testify that if a man deals with them justly and affectionately no mother can be more self-sacrificing towards her child than they are to the European in his need. Their courtesy to ladies is worthy of high-born gentlemen. Their loyalty to the white man who has shown consideration for them is deeper than a Highland clansman's for his chief. No native will allow his European master to come to any harm if he can prevent it, for he knows that not only will his own heart condemn him, but the village conscience and his chief will hold him guilty, and he will be accountable to them.

Man's Gratitude to Man

I have listened to the stern rebuke of a village headman who heard that in swimming a swollen river I had been carried away, and had been in some danger until rescued by my carriers. And he would not leave me until I promised never again to attempt so rash a deed.

One dark night when my wife and I were passing along a rough road near a village, I heard the chief who was walking in front call to the men behind: "If any of you let the Dona fall, I'll kill him." A wild enough threat for a stumble for which she alone would be responsible. For the men's sake, more than for her own, she had to walk warily.

Next morning the men rigged up a hammock with a pole and blanket, and, leaving some loads behind, carried me forty miles home to my station.

We arrived in the dark and as we passed through the wood the men in front met a number of villagers. The strangers were from the village of our sick headman. They had heard that their "Father" had been carried to Hora dangerously ill, and were travelling all night to be with him. They did not recognize me in the dark and began to upbraid my carriers in fierce tones for having deserted the sick headman. Then I spoke and their consternation

Man's Gratitude to Man

was as great as my resentment, which I also made them understand in cutting words.

That night as I lay in high fever, somewhere between two and three o'clock my bedroom door opened, and in stalked the neighbouring big chief and two or three of his *indunas*. He had heard that I had arrived ill and had risen at once and come to see how I was.

Next day I scribbled a note to my wife to tell her of my arrival, and unfortunately I mentioned my rough reception in the dark by the indignant villagers. That same day a messenger came from my wife with a letter to say that she was lying in high fever at Hora.

Here was a pretty mess. Her patient was nearing the crisis of his pneumonia in one room, while in another she was almost helpless with malaria, and I in the same condition forty miles away. But this was a type of the sudden crisis that may arise any day in this strange land, and we could do nothing but wait. A few days after I was able to sit out languidly on the verandah, and an hour or two after I got up my wife arrived smiling, with her patient following, both well on the way to a complete recovery.

Man's Gratitude to Man

When we were able to compare notes, she told me how she had staggered out of bed occasionally to see to her patient until he had passed the crisis. But while her fever was at its height my letter had arrived, and she was a bit unstrung with the wretched combination of evils, and had wept over the reception that had been given me as I neared my station. At this moment the head teacher looked in, and found her in tears. He asked what was wrong, and, hearing the story, he went out to the friends of the patient and gave them such a lecture as they had not had for long. Then he wrote to me rebuking me in fatherly fashion for my folly in sending bad news to my wife when she was ill. I could only plead guilty, and say that I was not aware of her condition.

The incident passed, leaving in both our minds a deeper sense of the bond of affection and consideration that ties us to the people whom God has sent us to serve.

Again and again, when days of dire stress came—and these are not unknown in lonely stations in Africa—we had occasion to test the loyalty and sacrifice of the humble folk about us, and we never found it fail. Swift journeys to summon help, when

Man's Gratitude to Man

runners travelled seventy miles in twenty-four hours, simple gifts to meet our need, for which no payment would be taken, solicitous consideration for the teacher when he was worn out with ever-multiplying claims, these and many another evidence of true hearts have bound us together by steel chains, and revealed the sympathy that runs through the brotherhood of mankind.

XV

MAGIC

THERE is no branch of mission service which wins so universal approval as that of a hospital scientifically and sympathetically conducted. There may be doubts about the wisdom of religious propaganda, and many distrust school work, but the philanthropy which has been created in everyone reared in a Christian atmosphere applauds all efficient effort made to save life and to relieve pain. The work, however, should be really efficient.

I once heard a famous Indian medical declare that " the Master had sent His disciples to heal the sick, not to humbug them with pills and powders." That there is a mighty lot of humbugging done by lay folk, out of goodness of heart, no one will dispute. For it is not easy to turn aside the trusting African, who gives every European credit for medical skill. And, of course, there is always the

Magic

hope that your Livingstone rouser, or dose of quinine, may not be useless.

But let us have as many qualified doctors as we can find and build for them as good hospitals as we can, for pain and death are all about us. And science is our St. George, who fights the dragon Magic most effectively.

Yet your science will not guarantee a splendid practice for you at once. You may be the only qualified doctor for a hundred miles on every side, and there may be thousands of sick all over the land, but do not suppose that you have only to put up your brass plate and light your red lamp, and the natives will fight for your Tono Bungay and keep your bell ringing night and day.

For you are not the only practitioner in the land, not by some hundreds, nor is your prestige anything like that of some of the mighty doctors and magicians who were first on the field. They have this great advantage over you, that they have learned long ago a fact never taught in your medical schools —that magic of some sort is at the back of nearly all sicknesses. Therefore magic must fight the battle.

You will suffer, also, by your absurd prejudices

Magic

against awe-inspiring trappings. In Britain you cultivate the " bedside manner," and when you have perfected it (not neglecting, of course, real scientific knowledge) the patients have faith and recover, and your bank account grows. In Africa the native doctor succeeds because of his excellent " bedside manner "—not, perhaps, the best type for the gentle English invalid, but the most appreciated by the African patient.

To ambitious beginners I would suggest these hints. Lay aside your pride and propriety, forget the British Medical Association and its etiquette, and open a real magic cave, with curtains, and skeletons, and curious lights, and blood-curdling sounds. Wrap yourself in a long coat, covered with cabalistic signs. Put a mighty pair of spectacles on your nose, and waving ostrich feathers in your hair. Dance a little, keep a vigorous jazz band behind the curtain, then dose with the vilest and stickiest mixtures you have, and I shall guarantee you record attendances and marvellous cures. Become a psychotherapeutist, and play on the nerves and emotions of your trusting patients.

The other day I saw a great native doctor at work, a sort of Harley Street specialist, who is called in

Magic

when the ordinary practitioner fails. I heard him
long before the village was in sight, for his drums
were calling, and the spectators were assisting with
song and clapping of hands. When I suddenly
appeared he became very shy, and gathered up his
drums and followers for a rapid flight into the bush,
leaving his fee behind. But I assured him, with
pleasant courtesy, that I should be most interested
to see his methods of work, and, with some vanity,
he resumed his interrupted treatment.

The patient was a daughter of the chief. She
looked very ill indeed, and for months had been
wasting away with a disease that had yielded to no
herbal medicine. Roots had been ground and
boiled, and she had drunk the concoction. Her
body had been cupped, and scarified, and anointed
with many a vile mixture. Snakes' teeth, rats' tails,
pounded bone, etc., had been bound about her neck,
her arms, her legs, in little magic bundles, but to
none of these had her disease yielded. Each new
doctor had been paid his fee before he supplied his
medicine. And, although clean, quiet treatment
might have been given at the mission hospital for
a fee of twopence, are not the roots of certain
shrubs, and the bundles of blessed magic, mightier

Magic

far than the little white and black pellets the European doctor administers?

Now the great *chirombo* specialist had been called in, and this is how he worked, for the *chirombo* he seeks is a little imp, elusive and malignant. The medicinal roots he carried with him were pounded and dropped into a pot of water standing on the fire, and the lid put over the pot. The miserable patient was placed before the fire and covered with a cloth, and told to inhale the steam rising from the pot.

" Should you feel something biting you, or an itchiness in your body, don't scratch. That is the *chirombo* rising into activity," Sir James had explained.

Cowering under her cloth, breathing smoke and steam, the girl sat rigid, while Sir James beat a drum behind her. Presently a shiver ran through her frame, and she began to tremble violently. " The *chirombo* has risen," cried the doctor. Now three or four others begin to pound small ear-splitting drums. The people who fill the hut break into song and rhythmical clapping of the hands, and the patient rises and essays a dance.

Wilder and wilder beat the drums. Sir James had

Magic

decked himself in coloured cloths, and breaks into a blood-curdling growl which he prolongs with mighty respirations. Several dancers have joined the patient; the rhythm and noise of song and hands grow swifter and swifter, until at last the patient sinks utterly exhausted to the ground. Two elder women seize her, stretch her hands above her head, and dance her up and down, rubbing her body and " straightening her out," as they say.

At length Sir James declares the first treatment to be over. He orders a goat to be brought, and it is held between him and his patient. The drums beat, Sir James dances, and then suddenly stabs the goat to the heart. Down drops the patient and, placing her mouth over the wound, sucks in warm blood. For to blood alone, and to no other medicine, will the *chirombo* yield.

When she has drunk sufficiently, the doctor orders the people to flay the goat. Part of the flesh is mixed with the medicine which is in the pot, and the patient drinks the soup thus made. The goat skin is cut into strips and hung about the neck of the patient. For a time she wears these, and while they cover her no one can visit her empty handed. A little gift must precede all conversation.

Magic

In the evening I passed that hut again, after Sir James and his apprentices had gone, having pocketed a good fee. The girl, with her mother, was sitting under the eaves of the hut, exhausted and quiet.

" Well, poor lassie," I said, " do you feel better now ? Has the great doctor cured you ? "

" He was beat," she said sadly ; " the *chirombo* would not yield to him."

" Wouldn't you come and try the mission doctor now ? " I suggested.

" It's so far away," was all she would say. But I knew her faith did not lie in that direction.

For *chirombos* are spirits, and they are divided into four or five classes, each requiring special treatment, and in all the shelves of the mission dispensary there is no medicine which deals with evil spirits. After all, what influence can a little pill have on an evil spirit ? It requires more special treatment and a peculiar language. So the girl will not come. Her disease is patent, and it is equally patent that the European has no medicine for such diseases.

For in Africa the master cause of all disease is magic, although there is probably no word in the vernacular just equal to this inclusive word. If the patient believes that magic is at the bottom of all

Magic

his troubles, who else can be his doctor but the magician, and that is why the Harley Street specialists in Central Africa are all " witch-doctors."

I once heard a dear old missionary from the far interior declare at a conference that the women of Africa in childbirth no more needed a doctor than the " hantelope on the 'ills." And I daresay that, in the majority of cases, the old gentleman's simile is very near the truth. But, alas ! for some young mothers, when the hour of darkness comes, and Magic is the only physician there !

Little Vukeya had married a strapping young chap. She was the light of his eyes, and he was as proud of her chocolate-coloured, rounded body and little hands and feet as ever husband was. The brass wire he gave her shone on her neck like a collar of gold. Her arms carried the gifts of his love in brass and ivory bracelets, and she had worked for herself the dainty bands of coloured beads that encircled her forehead. His pride in her had taught him to build for her the neatest house in all the village, and decorate it with coloured clays. With his own hands he had sewed for her reed mats, and carved her pounding mortar and her wide-lipped spoons.

All the village knew how deeply they loved one

Magic

another. For in the evening no whiter maize porridge was laid at the feet of the man by the kraal gate than that she laid in shining black porringer, accompanied by a little dish of tempting relish. True, she never ate with him. She would have been ashamed to do so. But the pride in his eyes was plain to all men when he glanced down at her gift to the common mess.

In public they seemed to have nothing in common. He talked with the men in his leisure time by the kraal gate, while she went with the women to the well, and pounded her maize, and prepared her food along with them. On Sundays when they went to church he walked with the men and sat along with them on their side, while she followed with the women and worshipped along with them. She had not even taken his name when she married, but he had paid a whacking dowry for her, and she had left her kith and kin and become, with all the off-spring that might follow, the property and possession of her husband.

If you would know the real community of spirit between these two souls, listen to them talking as they sit under the eaves of the hut in the evening, or join them round the bright wood fire on which

Magic

a little pot sits bubbling and gurgling with promise of some delicious relish.

But husband and wife cannot always be together in this land. The labour market is far away, and money must be found to pay the taxes, and to buy more bright clothes for the pretty wife, and to provide the luxuries which make life more dignified. So the husband has taken his load of meal, and some extra clothes, and is off to the plantations. A year, at least, will pass before his wife will see him again.

Now, while he is far away, the time of her trial has come. The husband's relatives are there, and the house is full of women. Two days have passed, and the child has not been born. Vukeya is worn and frightened, and the kind looks about her have changed to black suspicion. Hour after hour two old women have been urging her to confess the names of her guilty lovers. No one doubts that she has been unfaithful, else why this trouble and delay? Pains and terror are over her, but no look of sympathy greets her.

" Confess," they cry, " or you will die." But she protests her innocence, and begs for help. " Confess," is the only answer. Then someone, who is no friend of her husband, says, " It is he who

Magic

has done this. Far away at the plantations he has sinned. Now his wife is suffering for his sin." Then, as the wife knows in her heart that she is innocent, she asks, " Can it be he who has brought me to the edge of death by his unfaithfulness ? " The hours come and go, and death seems to draw nearer. She curses him in her heart for what he must have done, for all the pain and threatening death brought to her.

There are sounds of angry dispute without the hut. The whole discussion can be heard. It is the old elder of the church urging the absent husband's brother to take the poor young wife to hospital. The old women will not have it. She has not yet confessed her adultery, and unless she does she will die—nothing can save her. Compel her to confess. They have named a dozen men, but she will not charge one. At length the brother-in-law yields to the persistent pleadings of the elder. A hammock is procured, and two or three men carry her to hospital. A string of women follow. As soon as they arrive, the lady doctor and nurse appear. The young woman is made as comfortable as possible.

" When did this begin ? " asks the doctor. Slowly and with many a twist of prevarication the

Magic

story is told. You can see the fire kindling in the doctor's and nurse's eyes. The gentle ladies would flay alive Dame Magic if they could.

But this is no time for idle resentment. Kettles are on the fire. There is a quiet running to and fro. And then to the terrified friends in the waiting-room comes the sound of a little child crying, and the merry laugh of the doctor. Hands are shaken, and rounds of snuff precede a general exodus.

An aftermath of hate awaits the husband's return. The doctor has explained it all as reasonably as she could, and all she says may be true enough for European women, but in Africa things happen differently and suffering comes because of the offence of one. The wife knows that she was not guilty, therefore the husband must have been. She is sure that he has been unfaithful, and hates her, and has brought all this terrible suffering upon her.

At last he returns and the neighbours tell him all about those dark days. Then he despises and hates little Vukeya, who pretended to love him, and all the while played fast and loose with many loves· For he knows that he was not the guilty one, therefore his wife must have sinned. For all through the generations it was known that this trouble comes because of unfaithfulness.

Magic has sown her dragon's teeth in that once happy home and the years that come will bear the crop of hate and quarrelling and finally desertion. Magic has played her part in primitive society, by her terrors guarding property, and authority, and social order, and compelling temperance and abstinence. But when she has sat on the judgment seat, she has been a mad judge, unable to distinguish the innocent from the guilty, and hopelessly punishing the wrong party. More crimes lie to her charge than to passions.

XVI

CENTRAL AFRICAN VIGNETTES

A BREAKFAST ON THE SANDS

IN THE LOANGWA VALLEY.

DEAR ——,

I would not exchange with yours the life that I am now living here in Central Africa. Of course it is easy to draw a picture of what we do that would make our lot seem miserable enough and even sacrificial and heroic. To the eyes of some such a picture would be quite true. But it would not be true to mine. You can imagine what different versions could be given of how we spent pouring wet days in our little house in Arran. The children's memories of these days are as bright as any, and I would like to have something of the child's spirit when I tell you what I am doing now.

You started for your office this morning after a comfortable breakfast, and in half an hour an express train ran you out from the Ayrshire hills into the din and darkness of the city. I struck camp at five o'clock this morning in a dirty little village, and after a cup of cocoa, drunk amid the din and bustle of tying up tent and loads, started off. It has taken me five hours to tramp less than the distance you covered in half an hour.

The morning was pleasantly cool and we moved along at a good pace through leafless woods. We have seen no villages and passed no travellers, for we are now on that barren stretch which runs down to the Loangwa Valley, bound on a visit to the Senga. Twice we sighted game through the trees. The first were some large antelope, standing on the hillside, staring at our caravan, their coats shining bright in the morning sun. Again a troop of zebra, whose stripes looked very conspicuous in the strong light, in contrast to the burnt and blackened earth. But we made no effort to follow them, for my men were loaded up with game that I shot the other day, and it was not tempting to carry more over that barren hot waste that lies between us and the next villages.

By nine o'clock the sun had become very fierce. There is no shade in these woods. The leaves have all fallen and the grass has all been burnt off by the tearing fires that swept the land a month ago. The path is very stony. Broken quartz makes trying walking for the African, but most of the men have made going easier for themselves by manufacturing sandals from the skin of an eland I killed for them. One of the men carries my water-bottle and every two hours I get a long drink that gives me new life. But the others, with their usual improvidence, carry no water and suffer from thirst and the intense heat.

At last we arrive at the river where breakfast is to be cooked. It seems nothing but a great bed of heaped sand when we get down to it. Not a drop of water is visible. But at the bend of the river-bed the men scoop up the sand and soon have a hole filled with water. A swarm of bees, numerous butterflies and buzzing insects take possession of the hole. So the men wait a little till the insects have satisfied their thirst and the water has settled, and then take long drinks with great grunts of satisfaction.

Now I lie full length on the sand in the shade of a great tree, waiting for all the loads to come in, and for my breakfast to be cooked. There is a pot of tea and a cold roast of reed-buck and a cold pudding, the remains of yesterday's dinner. True, I have no table or chair, but the river sand makes an excellent couch and table. There are no shining spoons and linen, no delicious milk, or more delicious porridge. But there is hunger and the sense of a good long march accomplished to give most piquant sauce to the meal. Fifty yards away the men have kindled a fire and are preparing their maize porridge and roasted meat with a great clatter of tongues. The weary march is forgotten in anticipation of the meal that is preparing.

The river bed is frizzling in the heat. Sometimes a bird's note, full fresh and liquid, comes from the great trees that fringe the banks, and one is immediately transported to shady groves and tumbling waters.

Little flies keep up a restless buzz about me, and butterflies flit over the sand in scores. The heated air is rising from the river-bed with a wavy shimmer, as it does from over a fire at home. But in the shade of the trees where I lie it is comparatively cool. A honeybird has found us out and is chattering in great excitement, trying to make the men rise and follow it. But they will not move, and shout most ribald remarks to the friendly little scout.

You will now be rising from your office, with its window looking into the narrow lane, and you will go to have your lunch in some modern restaurant with rows of shining tables and smart waitresses and a band playing. But I would not exchange your seat for this one on the soft sand, nor your music for the sounds of hot, tired nature about me, and the song of the water that the bird is singing, nor your electric light for the glare of the fierce sun and the pale cool light of the moon in which I shall sit this evening outside my tent door, while the village children caper and play around. . . .

CHITIMBE THE HUNTER

Chitimbe has been a great hunter in his day, though now he seems a modest and inconsequent little fellow. When you ask him about his " kills," he will tell you accurately the number of elephants, rhinos and buffaloes that have fallen to his gun in any country, and just where he got them, but all the other antelopes of greater or less degree he sums up in a general catalogue, " and also game of no account."

To-night he has been sitting in my tent with two of his sons, and our talk has been very intimate. I have been in a good listening mood at the end of a long day of travel and school inspection, and my old guest has been more communicative than usual, for he has been telling me with much detail the simple and strange story of his coming to Christ. If I could get the full picture of all the adventures that led him into faith, the story should be exciting enough, though the mental processes are as simple as can be. But the setting of all the incidents was given in a series of quick movements of the hand and of little explosive particles, that conveyed a world of meaning to his sons, but only a dim outline to me.

Sixty years ago he was born near Bwabwa, the lovely hill whose changing colours the Ekwendeni station is ever watching. When he was still a boy the Ngoni armies arrived, coming out of the north. Before them his father escaped with his family to the lake and lived there for a while " eating fish." But soon the marauders swooped down on their hiding-places and again they fled, this time to

Central African Vignettes

Parausenga Mountain, in the west, a hundred miles away. But no peace was found there. The Ngoni came upon the stockade where they were living, and the father was killed in the gardens without. The stockade, however, was not entered.

Finding no safety in the west, they fled two hundred miles to the south. They had scarcely settled there when their restless enemies were upon them. Now they moved north, and in their new settlement learned how some of their clan had found rest by submitting to the Ngoni and being incorporated in the tribe. As there seemed to be no place where they could live quietly, they decided to yield themselves up and become slaves of the stronger people.

When Chitimbe reached manhood he entered the ranks as a fighter and went forth with the " impis." The last raid he took part in was against the Arabs in the north-west. He had now become an elephant hunter. Armed with an old gun and powder bought from the Arabs, he seems to have had not a little success.

Twenty-two years ago the mission opened a school in his village, and there he heard some simple things about the gospel. Light began to creep slowly into his soul. This is how he described it :

" I looked about me and said, ' Who made this great world and its big variety of living things ? There are the cattle and the hens, the elephants and the guinea-fowl. And here am I myself, and these are my finger nails. Who can have made these things ? No man has the skill to do it.' Then I saw it was God, and I began to believe that there is a God."

About this time he joined an elephant-hunting party that had entered into partnership with some Arabs, and they crossed Lake Nyasa together. He took no magical medicine with him to help to kill the elephants, and no charms to find out the magical sources of sickness. The other hunters laughed at him and said, " You will be a failure." But he answered, " There is a God. Let us see whether He is more able to help me than your charms are."

It was a long expedition. They followed their game far to the east along the Rovuma, and only turned when they were within two days' march of the Indian Ocean. One day the party was starving. Chitimbe started out alone to look for game, and meeting with a buffalo killed it with a single shot.

Central African Vignettes

They ate the flesh, and calling the villagers fed them also. Then my friend stood up before the Arabs and his fellow-hunters and said, " Now, who saved you from starvation? Was it God, or your charms?" Throughout that hunt all the luck seemed to be with Chitimbe. Four good elephants fell to his gun, one of them a huge solitary bull. Another little one he speared alone. So he turned his face homewards, saying, " There is a God."

They recrossed the lake in a big canoe. Midway a terrible storm came down upon them. The canoe filled with water, and every moment they expected to perish. The hunters cried out, " We are lost. We have died already." In the storm, Chitimbe remembered the story of Jonah as he had heard it in school, and he said to himself, " I am the man who is trying to escape from God." So he prayed, and prayed. Presently the heavens brightened, and the storm passed, and they landed in safety on the west shore. As he stepped out of the canoe he said, " God has delivered me, and the canoe has been the belly of the whale for me. When I shall get home I shall renounce polygamy and follow Christ."

But when he got home the sweets of the old

GWAZI AND A FRIEND

Gwazi on the right. The sunlight on her face deprives her of the refinement of feature which is her characteristic.

COOKING

A girl cooking maize porridge, she holds the earthenware pot with her toes. She wears brass-wire necklet, and lead disc earings.

life were too attractive, and he did not fulfil his vow.

Soon afterwards he was hunting with others in the thick bush. They were following the track of buffalo. Suddenly he heard the report of a gun, and ran to see where the shooting was. In his hurry he stumbled into the shade of a big tree, and fell against a great male lion that was resting in the shade. The lion rose up, pushing him as it rose. Its mighty mane was all over his chest, and it roared into his face. With a disdainful shove it cleared away, doing him no harm. He had no feeling of terror. But as the beast bounded off he said, " Indeed there is a God. Again He has delivered me. I shall fulfil my vows."

So he returned home, dismissed his second wife, and publicly confessed Christ. That was twenty years ago. " Where is your second wife ? " I asked.

" She married another man. She too became a Christian. She died a few years ago, leaving her two children with me."

" And what about your present family ? "

" God has greatly blessed me. I have seven sons and daughters, all with me. Two of my sons are teachers, and four of my children are married."

That night I met the catechist, and asked him if he knew the story of Chitimbe's awakening. "Yes," he said, "we all heard it long ago at the time of his conversion, and often since. God has many ways of revealing Himself to men."

ONE OF GOD'S SAINTS

I am spending a week-end in one of our distant churches holding special services. There lives near by, perhaps four miles off, one of God's dear saints, an old woman, whom I wish you may know. As I passed near her village on Friday I stopped at the school on the outskirts. The inquirers' class was gathering, and I said to the catechist :

" How is Grannie Gwazi ? " (I shall not attempt to spell her name correctly to home readers, for there is a " click " in it.)

" She has been ill for some time," he answered.

" Then I shall go to see her."

" Oh ! you need not. She will be here as soon as she hears of your arrival."

Central African Vignettes

" But she must not get up if she is ill," I said.

" Do you suppose she has missed a single meeting since she became ill ? Not one."

So I hurried off to prevent her rising to meet me, but was just in time to see her leaving her mat, where she had been lying in the sun. She looked very frail, a bent frame of bones. As she put out her two hands to welcome me, her face shone with that wonderful refined smile that constantly lights it up.

You see her often sitting so still and grave, and then the smile passes over her face like a gentle breath of wind rippling the water of a quiet lake. I suppose God has been whispering to her.

After her warm greeting, she lifted up her hand to heaven and blessed me. " Here comes the teacher of the Lord. Lord of hosts, clothe him with power." And then she shook me by the hand and laughed.

We all know her blessings. When the trader passes, or the Government official, she goes out to meet him, and blesses him, and before he rises to go she stands over him and prays for him.

" I am afraid you are ill, grannie," I said.

"Of course I am. See how thin I am. But sickness does not separate me from the love of God."

As I was leaving I said : "We shall all be sorry that you won't be able to come to the Communion. Might I send my rickshaw for you?" I added, knowing her intense desire for these services.

"No, no!" she cried, "don't send the rickshaw. I'll hirple along." And as I turned out of the village I heard her cry again : "Don't send the rickshaw. I'll hirple along."

I fancy that nothing but death itself will keep her back from her Communions, and then she will drink new wine in the Father's Kingdom. Not many years ago she swam a flooded river to attend the Sacrament at Njuyu. Her fellow-villagers stayed on the other side, afraid to cross. But when the meetings were over her courage failed, and she would not venture back till the river went down. Her desire to be present had made her laugh at the terrors of the torrent.

On Saturday morning I was sitting with the elders in the little vestry. Through the open windows there boomed the sound of many voices, scores of

Central African Vignettes

Africans greeting one another with "friendly yells," the shouts of children playing round the school. Suddenly a deep silence fell. All talk ceased, the children stopped their play, and there rose the voice of a woman praying in Chingoni.

"Gwazi has arrived," I said. For this is her usual way of announcing herself. She had hirpled along those four miles leaning on her staff. Now she stood in the open place before the church blessing the Lord of Hosts, and praying for the preacher and the people.

In the evening, when the sun had gone down, I was sitting at my tent door enjoying the cool, calm air and the wonderful colours of the sunset, when I heard the sound of someone singing. Presently out from the tall grass walked Gwazi, but she continued singing. Her song was a stately little chant, each clause ending up in a sweet little humming. It was a praise of the Lord of Hosts, and a prayer that He might never leave her. She swayed her body as the women do in the chorus of the dance, and now and then raised a thin, tapering finger to heaven, while the sweet smile lighted up her old queenly face. And so she continued until her song was finished, and then she blessed me and prayed for me, while I bent my head and received what she gave in the name of the Lord.

At every service on Saturday and Sunday she was evident, sitting near the platform, her weak back leaning against a big pillar. At the early morning prayer-meeting she was there, and took part, leading us in prayer. One could hear her, at each service that followed, punctuating the sermon with groans of appreciation when any truth touched her soul. Around her a score of old grannies sat, dear old ladies who are passing through the evening of their days in a sweet twilight, waiting for the opening of the everlasting day. With a strange reverence they cluster about her, acknowledging her as leader and mouthpiece of their worship.

When the Communion closed, and I had pronounced the benediction, Gwazi rose from her place and began to pray. It was partly a prayer, partly an exposition of the patience and faith of Job amid sufferings and tormentors, and all ending with a call to come to the feet of Jesus.

I went along in the evening to the elder's house where she was staying, and found her lying down very tired.

Central African Vignettes

" I'd like to hear again that song you sang at my tent," I said to her.

She was very shy, and fingered the border of her cloth like a timid girl.

" You may hear her in her own village every day at sunrise and at sunset singing these hymns," whispered the elder.

They have an echo of the old music the men sing to their *gubus* in the wakeful hours of the night. But they are her own—her own music, and the voices of her own soul.

Suddenly she broke forth. All the village could hear her as she sang again in a strong voice, her hand raised now and then to God, and the wonderful smile breaking over her face like the light of another world. All other village sounds ceased, the heathen sat quietly under the eaves of their huts, the children stopped their play. And the voice of the old saint praising rose and fell.

She is eccentric, very, if the fashion of this world is the centre. But there is no eccentricity in her to whom God is centre and heaven is home.

I see her nearing the Lord of Hosts, and His light breaking on her.

" Good night, grannie," I cried. " You'll soon

be singing a new song with the angels, and looking on the glory of the Lord of Hosts."

And she smiled, and blessed me in the name of the Lord of Hosts.

SONG AND VISION

It is Saturday night. For three weeks I have been travelling through the villages of this section, visiting a school daily, giving to the people some little morsel for their nourishment, and encouraging the teachers. Now we are nearing the close of our little tour. We are camped at Chasefu, on the borderland of the plateau, just before it falls away to the great Loangwa plain. Here some day, soon, I trust, we shall see a European station. I hoped to have found it already rising when I returned from Europe. But in God's plans, so mysteriously patient, the missionary who came to start it was invalided home before ever he had opened the work. Yet, in His good time, we shall find the man who will care for this large section of Northern Rhodesia.

I have been holding meetings here for a day or two, and numbers of Christians have gathered from the Senga country down in the valley, and from the villages of the plateau. To-morrow we shall celebrate the sacraments, and on Monday arrange for the opening of those thirty Senga schools where we try to keep the Lamp of God burning.

To-night I am sitting outside my tent in the light of the moon. Four or five catechists are with me. We have been talking together about their work and experiences, and they have been telling me, with all the glow and love of those who have just entered on a new and fascinating service, something of their efforts and difficulties. David has been stating at some length a little problem of his, and stops to ask Jeremiah, his senior, whether it is not so. But Jeremiah makes no answer. He is sitting with bent head listening to something else.

" What do you think now ? " again asks David.

" Oh," says Jeremiah, with a start, " I'm afraid I did not hear you. I was listening to the singing."

So were we all ; no one more than I. A hundred yards away, forty or fifty Senga teachers were singing together, " Nearer, my God, to Thee."

I had heard nothing else for some time. I was

away back on the hot plain in one of those early excursions, trying to tell for the first time of a Name, the Name that is above every name. I saw again the filthy stockades with the skull-crowned poles ; the timid dark souls whose only worship was about those shabby little erections for the spirits of the dead that stood in the clearing of the thicket. I saw again those days when I was the first to speak to them of God and Christ.

The years have passed since then, and by the feeble efforts of native teachers—ah, so feeble and so unskilled !—the lamp has been lit and kept trimmed and burning. Dimly enough at times—for strong winds of superstition have swept the valley, and sometimes the countless moths and insects of sin (so characteristic of the plain) have gathered about the light and almost smothered it. But it has been kept burning, and more and more lamps have been lit.

Now these Senga lads have come up to the plateau, and are singing together in the moonlight, " Nearer, my God, to Thee, nearer to Thee." I know that to others the music may sound harsh and untuneful. The harmonies are not correct. I suppose the air itself is wrong. But to-night I hear

no discord. I hear redeemed souls, to whom something of the glory and love of God has come, singing
a song of holy desire. And the village is full of
heavenly music. My Ngoni carriers have drawn
near, and are standing listening to the Senga. Some
of the visitors, too, are there. Other sounds have
ceased. All the little village groups seem to be
listening.

> " Like as the hart for water-brooks
> In thirst doth pant and bray. . . ."

The hymn has changed. Now it is the forty-
second Psalm :
They are singing it to the old tune " Glasgow." I
am back now in my father's Highland church. It
is a Sabbath afternoon, and the Spirit of God fills
the place. The congregation is sitting, singing this
psalm ; every note and trill of the old tune throbs
with the call of souls for God. I see one elder, his
head thrown back and his eyes closed, singing with
his soul in his voice. Last time I was home he was
there in church, whiter and older, but with the
thirst for God lighting up his face. The whole
congregation is before me this night in Central
Africa—men and women with a long tradition of

Central African Vignettes

Gospel preaching, jealous, too, for the ways of their fathers.

> "My soul for God, the living God,
> Doth thirst: when shall I near
> Unto Thy countenance approach,
> And in God's sight appear?"

It is not the old Highlanders, with their long traditions and their whitened hairs, that are singing; it is my black Senga lads, and the music is even sweeter from them than from the old Highland saints. I don't think any of them have searched so far into the wonder of God as the old elder. They have only now come from their dry, parched land to stand by the edge of the boundless sea of love and try its limitless depth and breadth. But God has come to them, too.

My imagination is off, galloping along another path, fired with the tremendous joy of pioneering. Yesterday and to-day I have been looking around to see where the European station may be built. I have found a place which I think is nearly ideal. It is a little rising, with a flat top, and the ground falling away on all sides. Tall shady trees cover the whole site. A short distance away is a stream of water, flowing from springs in a rich little valley.

Central African Vignettes

I see the station rising, with its dwelling-house and various little workrooms, its school and its pretty little church. I see the garden blossoming beside the springs of water. I think of the frequent tours along this plateau ridge and over that great fascinating valley. I see the little congregations of believers appearing in each one of these villages. What a privilege to be allowed to open and to control this work, and claim these tribes for the Saviour!

Where shall we find the man to whom this task may be given? For sixteen years we have waited, and yet he has not come.

Suddenly I hear Grahame shout, " Moderator ! " and I am in the Assembly Hall looking down on a great company of the saints and ministers of the Church, through whose silent standing ranks a simple procession is moving to the platform.

What a mass and power of service is there. It awes me to look at it. There are men who have grown old in the most glorious service man was ever called to. There are elders who amid all the pressure of business still place the Kingdom of God first. There are young men, in their neat clerical garb, who have just entered the great service. With

Central African Vignettes

God in them, what may they not yet do for Him and His world? Now I see the white-haired precentor stand forth to lead the singing. The song has started with a new volume: "Oh! happy day, that fixed my choice." Ah! this is no Assembly song. It is my Senga children, standing in their new morning, and rejoicing in the light that has come.

Here in this little African village, as the dark group, sitting and standing about that log fire, sing hymn after hymn, what thrills, and joys, and thanksgivings come to me! What music on earth is so tuneful? You may hear it when it is given to you to be the first to bring Christ to a people that sat in darkness, and then to hear them praising in the joy of their discovery of Him who has sought and found them.

I suppose I am dreadfully emotional. Well, there are emotions that come sometimes upon a missionary such as the angels feel in heaven over sinners lost and found.

I have seen Dr. Laws, in council, try to tell how this man whom we are about to ordain to the holy ministry first heard of Christ and found Him by his lips—but he could not. I have heard Dr.

Central African Vignettes

Elmslie, in a conference of missionaries, tell of the dark days in Ngoniland, and how the light came, but he sat down silent, unable to say it, and that was the greatest speech I ever heard him make.

Central African Vignettes

To-day I have been filling up, with rebellious feelings, schedules of figures for the Annual Report, writing up the balance-sheets of income and expenditure, of native liberality and costs of agents.

As the evening fell, and the last of these misleading or tongueless figures were filled up, I folded the papers with a sense of futility and falseness. For figure values here are so different from anything the reader at home will put on them. Twenty shillings is not the measure of one pound in a land where labourers earn twopence a day and teachers six shillings a month. What content will you put on one hundred baptisms, when each soul has its own history, and each is beyond price? What record of the Kingdom is there in a thousand church members, each differing from the other in light or darkness, in life or dead formality?

The figures I have entered are great and small. We play with hundreds, where the Indian missionary would thrill with tens. We count the pennies, where you at home would look for gold. Probably

Central African Vignettes

no one but myself will read these figures. But if some curious soul should glance his eye along the columns which are supposed to record the progress of the Kingdom of God, he will not read them in my language. Should they speak to him at all, their tongue will utter different things from what they say to me. I hear each figure tell a little—but at the best how little—of breaking light, of liberty and faith, of dull and joyless formalism, too, of growth and backsliding, of grateful giving and selfish withholding, of growing intelligence and of stolid ignorance.

There is a record of 2800 members in full communion, of 84 removals, of 870 baptisms. These figures are a cinematograph to me.

I see again the countless interviews, so hurried and unworthy, with souls who would profess Christ, some still with no thought of the meaning of the step they would take, others full of a strong confidence in the salvation that has come to them. Then I see the great gatherings here in the church, or under the trees beside some village school, when a score of men and women shall be baptized into the Name. Next, those constant Holy Communions, always so quiet and refreshing, though they followed one another, Sunday by Sunday, in almost unbroken succession, when we took the Body and Blood by faith, and God fed us with His own Hand. But with these pictures there are always mixed the Session meetings, when we cleansed the church, and called before us those who had publicly betrayed their Lord, some still defiant, and others humble and repentant, praying to be received again.

Right in the heart of the year's film there always pass the great pictures of the Convention, the mighty congregations, five thousand souls at a time, the great seriousness, the growing response to the teaching of the Spirit, and then the glowing, triumphant thanksgiving at the close, before the people break up to return to their homes, with new visions, new covenants, and great joy.

The figures of native liberality give another film. Many a talk in church and at out stations, when, with constant reiteration, we called on the people to give to God what He had so freely given them ; to rise out of dependent childhood, and learn to help themselves ; to show by generous gifts their pity for those in darkness, and their value of the light that had come to them. Then the monthly

Central African Vignettes

visits of scores of deacons to the homes of the Christians—receiving, admonishing, nagging, too, that each may give a little. The little markets here and there, where zealous deacons try to barter for cash the foodstuffs and bracelets given by their people who would not, or could not, give money. And last, those meetings when the deacons counted their farthings and pennies and handed them over to the European, perspiring in their nervous apprehension lest some minute threepenny-piece or obscure farthing should have been lost in the rags which served for purses.

What pictures we see in the medical columns. The suffering children whom no medicine can cure, because of the neglect of ignorant mothers, or the havoc of native medicine. The worn and helpless patients who have been carried in, emaciated and dying with the diseases they have contracted as porters in the war. The patience and skill of doctor and nurse rewarded at last, in pain relieved, hope revived, life restored.

But if you could see the school film as I see it, and know what the great figures of scores and scores of schools and thousands of pupils really mean, I wonder whether you would rejoice, or be ashamed.

Central African Vignettes

There you will see no stately buildings, elaborate furnishings, scientific teachers, but only simple, primitive buildings, peopled by boys and girls, more clothed with dirt than calico, sitting on the mud floor, and taught by lads who have scarcely crossed the threshold of the house of Knowledge. There are children, girls especially, who for years have not passed beyond the primer. But there are others, too, brimming with eagerness and response, whose progress is only interrupted by the inability of the teacher to take them further. In these schools, could you see the souls of men upon the film, you would find the nurseries of life, superstition dissolving, the knowledge of God breaking, a great unthought-of world unveiling.

If arithmetic is to be the measure of progress, who will find for us a table for acts of mercy, and words and deeds of truth? If only we had a register to record deepening character, growing knowledge, faith, Christ-likeness! Or a balance-sheet, with columns on one side for indifference to pain, for cruelty, superstition, suspicion, for inertia and drunkenness and wantonness, and, on the other side, for tender solicitude, for reasonable confidence, for progress in grace, in sobriety and purity. Then,

Central African Vignettes

I think, we should not rebel so much against the annual statistics, for there would be a record, true and revealing, of how the world is moving on, slowly perhaps, and hirpling, but moving on to the light, and the Image of God.